Salvation Sermons

By

REV. A. B. SIMPSON, D.D.

With an Introduction by

REV. WALTER M. TURNBULL, D.D.

Originally published in 1925.

New, edited work © 2013 by TheBiblePeople.com
All rights reserved to this new updated version.
May not be copied, reprinted, or sold without permission.

All scripture taken from the King James Version of the Bible

CONTENTS

INTRODUCTION 5

CHAPTER I:
WHAT IS CHRISTIANITY? 7

CHAPTER II:
THE NATURE OF SIN 19

CHAPTER III:
THE OFFERING FOR SIN 29

CHAPTER IV:
SIN AND SALVATION 39

CHAPTER V:
REDEMPTION THROUGH HIS BLOOD 53

CHAPTER VI:
BACK TO CALVARY 63

CHAPTER VII:
THE GOSPEL OF JUSTIFICATION 77

CHAPTER VIII:
FREE GRACE 93

INTRODUCTION

THROUGHOUT his ministry of over half a century, Dr. A. B. Simpson was unswervingly loyal to the Gospel of salvation through the vicarious atonement of the Lord Jesus Christ. His first pastorate witnessed a gracious work of the Spirit of God among the unsaved. In Louisville, Kentucky, he was largely instrumental in bringing about one of the mightiest revival movements that ever visited that city. So strong was his passion for the neglected and lost that in New York he relinquished his prominent pulpit and the congenial fellowship of a thriving church to begin aggressive evangelistic effort among the unchurched masses of the metropolis.

The Gospel Tabernacle, which became the center for his later activities, was largely built up through the conversion of men and women under his own ministry. His last public address was an impassioned gospel appeal to the soldier boys in Camp Merritt. His yearning was ever for the lost, at home as well as abroad, that he might by all means save some, and he was never happier than when he was used of God to lead a sinner home.

Because his messages on other phases of Christian truth were rather startling to his generation, they were more widely discussed than his great evangelistic addresses. Also, it was his duty, as a prophet of neglected truths, to emphasize those doctrines which had dropped out of the church's teaching and experience. Thus his best-known books and articles have been those devoted to the presentation of the deeper truths of the Christian life. This volume is therefore offered to the public with much satisfaction, since it will continue an important ministry of Dr. Simpson which hitherto has not been made sufficiently prominent in his published writings.

The addresses which are here gathered together were delivered at various times to large popular gatherings and were instrumental in leading many hundreds to Christ. The reader will sense in them the loving heart and deep sincerity of this great man of God.

Much blessing should follow this little volume which sets forth the fundamental truths of redemption so clearly and attractively. In the midst of much discussion about the veracity and authority of the Bible and of questioning regarding the historic doctrines of our faith, these powerful sermons will bring a timely message. Those who love the pure Gospel of Christ will welcome a book which may be safely placed in the hands of the young or passed to the spiritually troubled with the assurance that it will always point to "the Lamb of God which taketh away the sin of the world."

W. M. TURNBULL

CHAPTER I

WHAT IS CHRISTIANITY?

"Then Agrippa said unto Paul, Almost thou persuadest me to be a Christian"
(Acts 26:28).

WHAT is Christianity; rather, what is it to be a real Christian? Measured by statistics, there are several hundred millions of Christians in the world. Measured by spiritual dynamics, these figures would shrink to perhaps one-tenth or less of that estimate.

What is God's test of actual Christianity, the test of the Bible, the test of judgment, the test of reality?

1. Christianity is not an ecclesiastical matter. It is not settled by enrollment, baptism or confirmation. It is not a question of heredity or profession. It is as true of Christianity as it was of ancient Judaism: "He is not a Jew, which is one outwardly; neither is that circumcision, which is outward in the flesh: But he is a Jew, which is one inwardly; and circumcision is that of the heart, in the spirit, and not in the letter; whose praise is not of men, but of God."

2. Christianity is not a creed. It is not a set of correct doctrines, honestly believed and consistently proclaimed. It is not a matter of intellect, conviction and illumination. It is not the deepest and highest knowledge of divine things and even the ability to present them to others with truth and even persuasive power. We may have all these and yet be utterly destitute of personal religion. The seal of the religion of Jesus Christ is not the intellect, the imagination, the mind. It is not mental science or orthodox faith. It is something deeper, higher and more divine.

3. Christianity is not morality. It is not the reformation of bad lives and the conformity of our conduct to the highest ideals of duty and righteousness. All this may be accomplished by purely human resolution and endeavor. Heathen Greece and Rome had their ethical systems and their good men, but they were as far from the revelation of God as a torchlight is from the sun. Christianity includes right conduct and is the strongest force for reformation and righteousness, but its effect may be simulated by other causes. Judaism was founded, to a great extent, on moral law, and consisted largely in practical righteousness. But Judaism was not Christianity.

4. Christianity is not good works, zeal, benevolence, charity. All these may spring from other motives. All these may be but forms of selfishness, done from a desire to attain merit, or even from a natural impulse of kindness, and they may all exist without the grace of God. For the Apostle has said, "Though I give all my goods to feed the poor, and though I give my body to be burned, if I have not love it profiteth me nothing." And the word for "love" here is divine love, not the love of human impulse, but of divine creation. The records of patriotism are full of examples of heroic self-sacrifice. The religions of paganism are not lacking in

stories of self-devotion and the oft-repeated picture of the widow sacrificing herself on her husband's funeral pyre, the mother giving her very babe to the destroying arms of her idol god and the devotee of superstition giving up his life to self-inflicted torture and glorying in it as sincerely as the martyr dying at the stake for love of Christ.

5. Christianity is not devotion, prayer and worship. All these belong equally to the false religions of the world. There is no devotion more sincere and persistent than that of the shrines of idolatry and the altars of paganism. Even Cornelius, one of the highest types of heathenism in the best days of Rome, described by the inspired writer in the Acts of the Apostles as a man of generous liberality and habitual prayer, was not a Christian. For while the heavenly message that came to him declared, "Thy prayers and thine alms are come before God for a memorial," it was added in connection with his summons for Peter to come to him: "He shall tell thee words by which thou and thy house shall be saved." Certainly he was not yet saved, and his conversion to Christianity came when the Apostle brought him the message of Jesus and the baptism of the Holy Ghost.

6. Christianity is not feeling. There may be the deepest devotional feeling and the loftiest aesthetic emotion and devout fervor, and yet all this may be but human. Mere eloquence can stir the heart to tears and enthusiasm. The strains of music may wake up a thousand chords which seem like worship and devotion, and all this is frequently found in hearts and lives whose guiding principles are selfishness, worldliness and ungodliness.

What then is Christianity, if it be not intellectual, moral or emotional? Where is its seat? What is its source and how shall we find its touchstone?

Christianity is the religion of the spirit. Its seat is not the understanding, the conscience or the feelings, but that deeper province of our being that touches God—the spiritual nature. Christianity is a new spirit divinely created within us and united to the Father of Spirits, God Himself. It thus brings us into an entirely new word, as different from the intellectual and moral word as the difference between the scope of a human mind and that of one of the irrational creatures that surround us in the lower orders of animated nature.

The writer was once summoned to the deathbed of a lad who had been brought up amid the usual surroundings of culture and domestic affection, with a happy home and loving parents and friends, but without any religious teaching. For months his life had been wasting away while he kept clinging to the fond, fallacious hope of a possible recovery. At last the honest truth had to be told him, that he might not live another day. His family, who had dreaded to acknowledge the crisis, at last were forced to tell him. No spiritual comforter had ministered beside his bedside, and his own immediate friends were helpless to tell him of a Saviour they did not know. The writer was sent as a friend of the family to break to him the painful message of his approaching death, and to perform some ministerial rites for his spiritual benefit. Never had he faced a more trying and perplexing responsibility. As he sat down by that bright young life, that was flickering out like a dying candle in its socket, and looked into the gentle face, it seemed to him almost cruel to torture him with the thought of the dark and gloomy grave. A few questions were asked, and it was soon apparent that the lad had no conception of the Bible or the Saviour, but had the usual notion of unawakened souls that it would somehow be all right because he had never done anything very wrong, and God was merciful and kind. How could that untaught mind be led to the knowledge of Jesus in the few hours or perhaps moments before his soul would certainly take its flight? The awful weight of the task drove the minister to silent prayer to God for help of the Holy Spirit to work the miracle of a soul's salvation.

Suddenly there flashed into his mind a simple illustration. A beautiful canary was singing in a cage just over the head of the lad, and his attention was called to the little pet, which he dearly loved, and then this conversation began:

"What a pretty bird and what a sweet song." "Oh yes," said he; "I love to hear it. It is my constant companion."

"But you cannot talk to it or make it understand your thoughts."

"No, because it is only a bird."

"You could not speak with it as you speak with me; you could not tell it of your pain and your anxiety about your future; you could not confide to it your heart's secrets; you could not call it a member of your family and treat it as you would your sister or your mother, and it cannot enter into the things we are now talking about, and the deepest interests of your heart and life?"

"Oh, no," said he; "because it has only the mind and heart of a bird."

Then came the application of the incident. "If you should die tomorrow," said the minister, "and pass into another world and find yourself in the presence of God and even in heaven, you would be unable to understand their conversation, their songs, their joy. You would be a stranger, you would be lost, you would be out of place. You would want to get away. You could not be happy, even in heaven, because you are not a member of God's family. You have not been born His child. You have not received the new heart 'that understands Him, loves Him and enjoys Him.'"

Suddenly it all flashed upon the mind of the lad and he saw eternity in a new light. Even if he had not done anything wrong, even if God was good and kind, he was incapacitated for the fellowship of God and for the happiness of heaven just as the little bird was for his fellowship, because he was without a spiritual nature. He had his bodily life, which was soon to go out. He had his mental life, which would continue in immortality, but he was without spiritual life, and his face became distressed with a look of anguish, and he cried:

"What shall I do? They tell me I cannot live, and I see that I am not prepared to die. How shall I receive this new nature that I have never known?"

Oh, how easy it was to tell him now of the blessed work of Jesus and of His simple loving word to another soul, one night, hopeless like himself: "Except a man be born again, he cannot enter into the kingdom of God; he cannot see the kingdom of God."

And then we told him that Jesus Christ came into this world just for the purpose of giving us this new birth, this new heart, this new spirit, that could know Him, love Him, enjoy Him and become His very child. We repeated to him such simple helpful words as these: "As many as received Him, to them gave He power to become the sons of God"; and, "Behold, what manner of love the Father hath bestowed upon us, that we should be called the sons of God." We told him that the very gift of Jesus that He was waiting to bestow upon anyone that would receive it was this new heart that could trust and love God, and then we asked him if he could not lift his heart in prayer to God and ask for his great gift through Jesus Christ.

Never shall we forget the moments that followed, the simple prayer, the tears that slowly trickled down the wan face, the intense concern that came over it as he closed his eyes and followed us in prayer. The simple prayer asked but one thing and claimed it because Christ had promised it, and then that strange "light that never shone on earth or sky" came over his face and told us that God had met him, that the miracle of grace had been performed, that a revelation had come to that dying boy and that heaven was opened to his soul before he entered it. It was unutterably real and beautiful, and as he opened his eyes and looked with that look of joy and then began to lisp out his first real prayer, we knew that the work was done. It was all so simple and brief, so real and oh, such a relief from a burden that had seemed to crush us, that we had not words to thank God for His precious grace. The conversation lingered a little longer, a few simple promises and counsels were added and then duty called us elsewhere with the promise to return in the morning.

As we hastened to keep that promise and approached the steps of the dwelling, a waving band of crape on the door told us that we had seen Arthur on earth for the last time. But the father met us in the hall, bathed in tears, and though an ungodly man himself, he was all broken and softened as he told us the sequel of that little visit. He said that the lad had lingered, very happy and peaceful, until late in the night, and they had left him for a little, he, the father, occupying the next room; and about the middle of the night he heard him talking as if to someone near. And then, as he hastened to his bedside, the little thin hands were stretched out as if to meet someone, and his voice was faintly speaking to someone that seemed near, and his face was lighted up with unspeakable joy. He seemed to be saying, "They are coming, they are coming, they are coming for me," and then he sank back. The spirit had fled. "But," said the father, "I have never believed much in these things, but it will be different now, for I know it is all true."

What was it that came to that dying lad? It was a spiritual experience. It was a new spirit; it was an element that had been hitherto lacking in his life; it was God revealing Himself to his spiritual nature and putting into him a new nature that could understand and answer back to the God that gave it. That is Christianity, in its germ. That is the new heart, which theologians call regeneration; that is something as different from human nature as a star is different from a candle's light; that is a new creation just as wonderful as the creation of the world.

And this new spirit grows, develops, unfolds and expands into all the possibilities of a divine and eternal life. It is this that becomes the dwelling place of God Himself. It is this that is united to Jesus Christ by the Holy Ghost and becomes the house of God and "the secret place of the Most High." It is this that becomes the predominant faculty and force of Christian life, dominating the mind as the mind dominates the body.

Its intercourse with heaven is immediate, instinctive and intimate. It knows God directly and by intuition. It is something like the intuition of the bird, which knows things, not by reasoning, but by an innate certainty that is in a sense supernatural and divine, at least a gift of God.

The spiritual nature has its senses like the physical. It hears the word of God, not in audible tone, but in unmistakable ways. It beholds the face of God and walks "in the light of His countenance," and there is an inner, higher and supernatural atmosphere as real to it as the warmth and light of nature's sun. It tastes the sweetness of God's loving manifestations and gracious gifts. Its language often is, "Thy words were found, and I did eat them; and thy word was unto me the joy and rejoicing of mine heart." It has the sense of touch and is conscious of contact with Divine Presence, of the approach of evil and of the spiritual channels through which life and healing come into the body. It can touch Him in a different sense from the jostling crowd in mere physical contact. It can say of Christ, "That which we have seen and heard, which we have looked upon with our eyes and our hands have handled of the Word of life."

And finer than all the rest, it has the sense of smell, that "quick scent in the fear of the Lord," which was the peculiar feature of the Master Himself, that instinct that scents both good and evil and discerns the "things that differ." To these spiritual senses God and heaven are very real, and the world to come is not a dream, but we are living in the constant foretaste of it and have already anticipated in our limited measure all that we shall enjoy in its larger fullness.

It is the absence of this spiritual life that constitutes the difference between the cultivated minds of earth and the humble and often illiterate but heaven-taught spirits to whom God has revealed Himself. "The soul man" is the literal translation of the Apostle's description of merely intellectual minds. Literally it is the psychical man, and of him Paul says, "He receiveth not the things of the Spirit of God, for they are foolish unto him; neither can he know them, for they are spiritually discerned." "The spiritual man judgeth all things [literally "discerneth all things"], yet he himself is discerned of no man." It is just like the simple figure that saved the dying boy. It is the difference between the canary and the child. The intellectual nature cannot grasp the heavenly world. We must have the mind of God, the Spirit of God, the nature of God, to know God and things divine. This is the key to the Apostle's strong language in 1 Corinthians 2:9–12: "Eye hath not seen nor ear heard, nor hath it entered into the heart of man, the things that God hath prepared for them that love Him. But God hath revealed them to us by His Spirit. The Spirit searched all things, yea the deep things of God. For what man knoweth the things of man save the spirit of a man which is in him? Even so the things of God knoweth no man, but the Spirit of God. Now we have received not the spirit of the world but the

Spirit which is of God, that we might know the things which are freely given us of God."

How vain for us, therefore, to expect the most brilliant intellects of earth to comprehend spiritual truth. The writer once called upon a distinguished lawyer, a member of his congregation for whom he had long prayed, and asked permission to talk with him about his soul. The lawyer listened politely for a while and then frankly said: "You may think it strange, but I really do not comprehend you. I can understand a proposition in business or the statement of a principle in law, but I do not even grasp your thought about what you call spiritual life and conversion. It is all an enigma to me. I cannot follow you." And he was perfectly frank and sincere.

Let us pray for such men, that God will give them a revelation of themselves and of Christ through the Holy Spirit. And let us thank Him, above all things, that it has been given to us "to know the mysteries of the kingdom of heaven."

And oh, if any reader of these pages is under the delusion that he can become a Christian at his own convenience and when he is ready can turn to God and get into heaven just as soon as he is tired of a life of sin, let him awake to realize that he is as helpless as the dead, that he is without God, without life and without power to create his own life. "As well might a man expect to pull himself up from the ground by pulling at his own boot straps" as to rise to God and heaven by his own efforts. No, dear friends, you are dependent upon a higher power, that very power that you are now slighting and despising. Oh, turn to Him in your helplessness and accept from Him that mighty, priceless gift of THE LIFE which He has come to bestow, and without which you must perish miserably and eternally in your helplessness and sin.

It is admitted that there is another side to Christian experience, a judicial aspect, by which the soul accepts the Atonement of Jesus Christ and is justified freely by His grace from the guilt and punishment of sin. But this is always coincident with the deeper spiritual experience just described. "If any man be in Christ Jesus, he is a new creation. Old things are passed away. Behold, all things are become new."

CHAPTER II

THE NATURE OF SIN

"By mercy and truth iniquity is purged"
(Proverbs 16:6)

"He that covereth his sins shall not prosper: but whoso confesseth and forsaketh them shall have mercy"
(Proverbs 28:13)

THE Bible's doctrine of sin is immeasurably higher than any of the conceptions of human religions. Men's religions either unduly excuse and palliate it or inexorably condemn it. Man's mercy would sacrifice justice and purity on the one hand, and on the other, man's justice and judgment have no place for mercy. The peculiarity of God's teaching about sin is that it measures its full malignity and guilt and at the same time provides for its forgiveness and removal with wisdom, love and power to which all natural religions are utterly a stranger. There is no weakness, soft indulgence or compromise in God's esteem of sin, and yet there is no sin too great for God to forgive and cleanse. The awful fact of sin has brought out something in the Divine nature which normal conditions never could have revealed. Like a great iceberg floating down the southern seas until it meets the Gulf Stream and that great and shoreless stream of warmth embraces the monster until it melts in dissolution, so Divine love has met the monster of sin and embraced it to death and left a new record in the government of God and the story of the ages, which wondering angels and ransomed men shall never fully comprehend. "Where sin abounded, grace did much more abound."

I. THE WORLD'S ESTIMATE OF SIN

"Fools make a mock at sin" (Prov. 14:9). The world holds virtue and righteousness at a low value and lightly scoffs at Puritanical precision and calls its forbidden pleasure and illicit indulgences sport, amusement, having a good time, or just a little bit of fun. Youth, temperament, temptation are allowed to excuse the most flagrant violence of purity and virtue, and it is almost taken for granted that every young man is expected, for a while at least, to "sow his wild oats" and play the game of fool and freedom, while conscientiousness, self-control and good morals are almost certain to be ridiculed as "straitlaced," "old fogy," "pharisaical," or "hypocritical." John Angell James tells that when he first left home to attend college and knelt down to pray at night before retiring, he was greeted with a whole fusillade of boots and shoes. But he stuck to his guns, and before a week ended, the attacks had ceased and one or two of the boys were praying with him. The man or woman that lightly jests about sin will find someday the laugh turned the other way and the comedy a tragedy of shame and sorrow. Let us be careful how we lower the standard of right and let down the bars of holy restraint. The most fearful feature of the devil's latter day religions, such as Christian Science and New Thought, is that they ignore sin. This is perfectly consistent with the devil's whole precedence. He began in Eden by mocking sin and saying, "Ye shall not surely die," and he has kept up his favorite lie all throughout the ages, until today he has some sweet name, some pretty phrase, some shrewd evasion or excuse for almost every vice and crime. Let us remember that the voice of God from first to last is intelligible, inexorable, that sin is exceedingly sinful and "the soul that sinneth it shall die."

II. THE UNIVERSALITY OF SIN

"Who can say, I have made my heart clean, I am pure from my sin?" (Prov. 20:9). This is the testimony of God's Word from beginning to end: "All have sinned and come short of the glory of God." "There is none righteous, no not one." From every age and from every land the testimony of human nature is the same. Man's conscience instinctively testifies to his sin. The burden of sin, the fear of punishment, cannot be charmed away by pleasure, poetry, art or philosophy. It is this that makes life miserable and death terrible, for "the sting of death is sin" and "the wages of sin is death."

III. THE LAW OF SIN

"The fruit of the wicked tendeth to sin" (Prov. 10:16). Sin is the natural tendency of all men. It comes out in the issues of life just as naturally as the fruit grows upon the tree. You cannot make a bad tree bring forth good fruit, and you cannot make a bad man do real good things. Divine religion, therefore, does not attempt mere reformation but goes to the very roots of character and demands and gives regeneration, and then it is true, "But now being made free from sin, and become servants to God, ye have your fruit unto holiness and the end everlasting life."

IV. THE SINS OF THE HEART

"The thought of foolishness is sin" (Prov. 24:9). The Lord Himself said, "Out of the heart proceedeth evil thoughts." Sin begins in a thought. "He that hateth his brother is a murderer." He that looketh upon a woman with unholy desires has already in God's sight committed the sin which may never actually materialize. The true self is the unseen man who stands behind the mask of your countenance and his thoughts, feelings, desires and purposes are all photographed and phonographing themselves every moment upon the tablets of eternity and the books of judgment.

V. THE SINS OF THE TONGUE

"In the multitude of words there wanteth not sin" (Prov. 10:19). Language is the embodiment of thought and gives it actual form and potential force. Your unspoken thought reaches no one but yourself and may harm no one else, but your words are winged messengers, winged arrows, poisoned arrows, too often, and they bring your sin into vital contact with other lives and kindle fires through the whole course of nature until at last your sinful tongue itself is set on fire of hell. Solomon must have heard and seen much of the curse of an evil tongue, for the book of Proverbs is crowded with pictures of this little member in all its manifold transgressions, the false tongue, the slanderous tongue, the backbiting tongue, the flattering tongue, the frivolous tongue, they are all here and their words are bitterness, destruction and misery. Well may the apostle say, "If any man offend not in word, the same is a perfect man, and able also to bridle the whole body." The first thing a physician asks of his patient is usually, "Put out your tongue," but just as truly is it the test of spiritual health and soundness of heart. Beloved, has God saved you from the sins of the tongue?

VI. THE SINNER'S WAY

"The way of transgressors is hard" (Prov. 13:15). The tempter may flatter and for a time the course of evil may be smooth, but at last every sinning soul shall find that God has spoken truly when He said, "Say ye to the wicked that it shall be ill with him." The transgressor is going in the face of nature, and he will find that sin is violence to the true order that God has made in His universe. Just as it is harder for that car with its wheels off the track than on, so it is harder to do wrong than right. You are sinning in the face of God's law, God's providence, your own conscience, your true happiness, the welfare of others and the final judgment of God, and you shall find at last you took the hard way. What a story the Bible tells, what a cloud of witnesses reiterated all along the way: Lot trying to enjoy the attractions of Sodom until at last smirched and well nigh consumed in its destruction; Achan enjoying for a few passing hours his worthless prize and then dying amid a shower of stones and leaving his name for a proverb and a curse; David turning aside from the path of virtue and overshadowing his glorious reign with a curse that never passed away; Solomon neutralizing all his matchless wisdom with the sin and folly that covered his closing days with shame and left a heritage of division and declension to his kingdom for centuries to come. And all aboard that long train that completes the progression of the broad road that leads to destruction, how they all unite as they pass out of sight to echo the same bitter cry, "The way of transgressors is hard."

VII. THE INEXORABLE RESULTS OF SIN

"His own iniquities shall take the wicked himself, and he shall be holden with the cords of his sins. He shall die without instruction; and in the greatness of his folly he shall go astray" (Prov. 5:22-23). What a striking passage, what a solemn picture! A man weaving the web that is to be his winding-sheet. A man forging the chains with his own hands that are to bind him in the dungeon of retribution. A man earning by his own toil the wages of death that are to be so fully paid. Wisely did the old colored woman say to the impertinent youngster who was laughing at hell and the impossibility of finding enough brimstone to make such a pit of sulphureous fire, "Oh, honey, they all carry their own brimstone with them." Sin is hell. Every time you do wrong, you create a habit that makes it necessary for you to do wrong again. Every time you wound your conscience, you lay up in store a fiery dart with which that conscience will smite you in the day of remorse and remembrance. No need for a flaming avenger to drag you to your doom. As naturally as the flood that rushes down the torrent will you find the level of your own place. There is nothing so terrible as for a man to wake up and find that he cannot stop sinning. Everlasting punishment is reduced to a very simple argument by the fact that it is just everlasting sinning. One is reminded of the bitter cry of a stage driver in the delirium which accompanied his fatal sickness after a life of awful sin. He had been accustomed to driving a stage on the precipitous incline where he had to use the brakes to hold his heavy vehicle. As his miserable soul was rushing down the more terrible incline of death, he cried out in dismay, "I am rushing on the downgrade and I can't get my feet on the brakes!" Oh, how many men are there today held by the cords of their own sins!

VIII. THE PROVIDENTIAL JUDGMENT AND RECOMPENSES OF SIN

"Behold, the righteous shall be recompensed in the earth: much more the wicked and the sinner" (Prov. 11:31). The full judgment of human lives does not come in this world, but there are terrible foreshadowings even here. How striking the testimony of a cruel king in a chapter of Judges. This wicked tyrant had just been captured and punished by a terrible judgment, and this was his bitter testimony: "Threescore and ten kings, having their thumbs and their great toes cut off, gathered their meat under my table; as I have done, so God hath requited me. And they brought him to Jerusalem, and there he died." How often that tremendous word has been fulfilled. "It shall be done to thee as thou hast done." "Judge not, that ye be not judged, for with the same judgment ye judge, ye shall be judged," and "as ye measure to others it shall be measured to you again."

IX. THE HARVEST OF SIN

"He that soweth iniquity shall reap vanity" (Prov. 22:8). This word "vanity" is a word of frequent use in the writings of Solomon. Again and again it is the final note in his dirge of disappointment over the failure of all earthly hopes, and "vanity and vexation of spirit." It speaks of the utter emptiness, hollowness, disappointment, failure and cruel mockery that come at last as the end of a wrong career. It may be long delayed, for the harvest does not always immediately follow the sowing, but it comes as surely as God has said, "Whatsoever a man soweth, that shall he also reap." And the reaping is always greater than the sowing. If you sow the wind, you shall surely reap the whirlwind. What if you do succeed in getting money? The money will fool you and fail to give you happiness. What if you do win honor and fame? They will prove a hollow mockery and leave you to cry as others have before, "I have everything and everything is nothing." What if you do win flattering friends? They will only have the greater power to deceive, disappoint and fail you. If there is sin in the foundations of your life, you may build as high as heaven and you may build with the costliest materials, but your edifice will fall and overwhelm you in its ruins.

X. THE REMEDY FOR SIN

"By mercy and truth iniquity is purged." The word "purged" is the familiar Hebrew word "to cover," so often applied to God's propitiation for sin. The allusion is undoubtedly to the mercy seat that covered the ark, and the broken law with its covering of blood, so that God did not see iniquity in Jacob or perverseness in Israel. Solomon introduces here two words that are comprehensive of the whole plan of salvation: mercy and truth. Mercy is that Divine love that loved us even when we were dead in sin and provided a great plan of redemption through Christ's atonement. Truth is the Gospel message which brings that mercy to us and enables us to believe it, receive it and be saved thereby. It is through the truth that we receive the Saviour and appropriate His covering of blood and righteousness. It is through the truth also that we are sanctified and more fully purged from the power of sin. God's Word searches and reveals every fault and stain and then leads us to the fountain of cleansing, the source of grace and power to purify, and saves to the uttermost.

XI. GOD'S FORGIVENESS OF SIN

"He that covereth his sins shall not prosper: but whoso confesseth and forsaketh them shall have mercy" (Prov. 28:13). This brings us still more fully into touch with the practical application of God's great remedy for sin. The chief hindrance to appropriating it is the covering of our sins. This expresses a great deal. We may cover our sins by lack of true conviction, by the absence of a sense of sin and an awakening of conscience. Or we may try to excuse and palliate our sins. God cannot save

The Nature Of Sin

us until we confess judgment and take the position so finely expressed in Romans, "That every mouth may be stopped, and all the world may become guilty before God." In courts of law, while the accused person pleads not guilty, the trial must take its course and the crime must be pressed home by all the force of the prosecuting attorney. But when the person pleads guilty, then mercy can interpose and at least lessen the severity of the sentence. And so we read of God's divine court of justice that "he hath concluded them all under sin that he might have mercy upon all." But we must unite with God in this conclusion before we can receive His mercy. For the Pharisee, there was no mercy, for he acknowledged no sin. To such people Christ can never be a real Saviour. We must meet Him on the ground of utter unworthiness and surrender. "But whoso confesseth and forsaketh them shall have mercy." Confession is practically giving up the contention and the defense. It is calling sin by its right name. It does not mean blazoning your past life before the world, but taking the place where God puts you of a guilty, hell-deserving sinner. Confession is to be made to man only where man has been affected by your sin and you owe the restitution, but you ought to confess to God all sin and so to confess it as to renounce all sins, evasion and self-complacency. Take the sinner's place and claim the sinner's Saviour.

But your confession must be echoed by practical righteousness. Sin must be forsaken. Repentance is more than sentimental sorrow. It is a change of mind, a change of will, a change of conduct, a change of direction in your whole life. It is facing the other way, turning your back upon sin and henceforth following after righteousness.

This at once puts the soul on the ground of mercy, and before you have felt any thrill or received any witness, you are already accepted, forgiven and saved by the simple change of attitude. And so we read of the publican who had taken this attitude, "He went home to his house justified." From the moment he took his right place, he was in possession of God's mercy and salvation. How very simple a Gospel this is. As a great statesman once said, "The way to get God on our side is to get on God's side." Who will get on God's side of sin, even as you read these lines, and have God forever on yours?

XII. OUR ATTITUDE TOWARD THE SINS OF OTHERS

"Hatred stirreth up strifes, but love covereth all sins" (Prov. 10:12). The grace that you have received will make you gracious to others. The pardoned sinner by inevitable necessity must be charitable, forgiving and tender toward his erring brother. Therefore, we find in the New Testament that unforgiveness is an unpardonable sin. This is not only true of your individual wrongs, but of all sin. The Christian is not permitted to sit in judgment upon the sins of others. We are not fit for this work. And God graciously saves us from it and reserves it for the judgment seat of Christ and unerring hands of His mighty angels who shall sever the wicked from among the just in the great separating day. If you have a spirit of censoriousness, of criticism, of searching out iniquities, of condemning, of evil speaking, of slander and backbiting, you know nothing of the Spirit of Christ and you will probably find someday that your own sins are not forgiven. There is no place where the conscience of Christians are so callous and blind as about this matter of judging one another. Our business is the love that "thinketh no evil" and that covers all sins. Oh, the wounds we cause the heart of Christ and the heart of our brethren by our lack of love, and the greater wounds we cause our own souls—bitterness, malice, calumny—are as the piercing of a sword to those against whom they are turned. But it is a two-edged sword, and the keenest wound is given to the hand that wields it. God, give to us the love that thinketh no evil, beareth all things, believeth all things, hopeth all things, endureth all things and never fails.

CHAPTER III

THE OFFERING FOR SIN

"Christ loved us, and hath given himself for us an offering and a sacrifice unto God for a sweetsmelling savour"
(Ephesians 5:2).

"He hath made him to be sin for us, who knew no sin; that we might be made the righteousness of God in him"
(2 Corinthians 5:21).

GOD gave His ancient people four great pictures and object lessons to illustrate the meaning of Christ's sacrifice for sin. These were called the burnt offering, the peace offering, the meat offering and the sin offering. From age to age these living object lessons were continually before their eyes as a sort of sacred drama in which they could as in a mirror behold the Lamb of God who in the fullness of time was to take away the sin of the world. As we look back to these ancient pictures, they give to us a spiritual interpretation of what God meant by that great sacrifice and they make the cross of Calvary more real and significant to us today.

I. THE BURNT OFFERING

This was the first of the great sacrifices of the ancient tabernacle. It represented the offering of Christ's life, love and obedience to His Father in our stead and as our righteousness. God had looked in vain for anything from man but sin and disobedience. In the world's first ages, so rank had been the ill savor of human violence and crime that God could stand it no longer, and by an angry deluge He swept the whole race away but a single family. The generations that followed were no better, and God pathetically cried through one of the ancient prophets, "I looked for a man among all their tribes, but I found none." At last, however, one Man appeared whose single purpose was to please and glorify God. Even in His childhood His testimony was, "I must be about my Father's business." And when at last He stood upon the banks of Jordan fully dedicated to His life and ministry, at length God looked down upon humanity with satisfaction and cried, "Behold My beloved Son in whom I am well pleased." That was all expressed in the burnt offering that the ancient priests continually presented upon the burning altars of the tabernacle and temple. There was no suggestion of sin. The entire body of the bullock or lamb cut into minutest pieces was offered up with frankincense and fire, and its fragrant smoke continually ascended as "an odor of a sweetsmelling savour." The idea suggested by the minute pieces was that every little act of the Saviour's life was one ceaseless offering of love. Thus He fulfilled all righteousness and presented to God an offering so perfect and acceptable that for His sake ever since, God can accept us unworthy sinners and bestow upon us the love and good pleasure which He feels toward His only begotten Son.

Dear friend, have you accepted this great offering as your righteousness, and are you continually presenting it to God as a ground of your acceptance and the inspiration of your love and consecration?

II. THE PEACE OFFERING

This was quite different from the burnt offering. It represented a feast in which the sacrificial lamb supplied the meal, and God and the worshipping priest met in fellowship and communion, both feeding upon the same precious lamb. The fat and the innards of the victim were given to God as His portion, and the right shoulder and the breast were given to the worshipper as his portion and as the first ascended to God from the altar in fragrant fire. The second was partaken of by the worshipping priests, and heaven and earth met around Jesus Christ and were reconciled, united and brought into fellowship and love. We must never forget that Jesus belongs to the Father quite as much as to the sinner. God feeds upon Him as His joy and delight, and we feed upon Him as our strength. The best part of Christ belongs to God, but to us He gives the right shoulder of His strength and the bosom of His love. How beautifully this is brought out in that significant verse, Rev. 3:20, "I will sup with him and he with Me." It is a joint feast when the soul is reconciled to God through Jesus Christ, a heaven below in anticipation of the heaven to come.

One is reminded of the story of a missionary among the Indians. He was going one day with his wife many miles along the frozen snow in his dog sled to visit a Christian Indian and his family and dine with him. He sent word to the Indian to prepare the feast with the best he had and be sure that everything was clean and ready. And then he and his wife filled up their sled with other provisions of which the Indian never dreamed. There was tea and sugar and preserved fruits and meats and real bread. When they reached the Indian tent, their host apologized for their poor fare, for they had nothing but dried fish. But they brought it out and spread it on a clean table, and they and their children were ready in spotless cleanliness to share the humble feast. Then the missionary brought out his feast until the table groaned under its weight of luxuries, and the humble people watched and wondered. Then they all sat down together and shared the bounteous supply. The missionary quoted Rev. 3:20, and told about the better feast of heavenly love in which we brought our best and God brought His best and supped with us and we with Him. That is what Christ's offering has brought us, fellowship with heaven, and a feast of love begun on earth and continued in the skies.

III. THE MEAT OFFERING

This was quite different from the others. Here there was no slaughtered animal, but just fine flour mingled with frankincense and oil and baked in unleavened cakes which were offered first to God and partaken of by the worshipping priest. This was intended to set forth not so much the death of Christ as the life of Christ as our Living Bread. Bread is quite the stuff of life. It is our commonest daily food. And the idea is that the humanity of Jesus Christ is given first to the Father as His portion and then to the Christians as the strength of His life. Christ said with reference to this, "He that eateth me shall live by me." Just as the mother gives her life to her babe, just as a close friend actually communicates to us a certain portion of his very being for our comfort, strength and joy, so in an infinitely closer and higher sense, the Lord Jesus feeds us with His very being and reproduces in us all the life which He Himself once lived on earth. Beloved, have we learned thus to draw our strength from Him and find Him, our stuff of life and Living Bread?

IV. THE SIN OFFERING

So far we have been looking at Christ without any special reference to His sacrifice for sin. If there was nothing else, we would have now before us the whole Gospel as the modern

The Offering For Sin

preacher loves to proclaim it. This is a Gospel without the cross, the precious blood and the atonement for human guilt and sin. Christian Science can accept all this without a murmur of dissent. The New Theology delights in this bloodless Gospel and loves to tell of Christ's beautiful life and heroic death as our example of noble living and self-sacrifice.

Yes, they say, Christ lived a beautiful life and died a noble death and taught us how to live and die. He is our perfect example; He is our sublime inspiration; He is our burnt offering, our peace offering, our meat offering.

But do not say anything about sin. Do not disturb the tranquility of our minds by any harsh insinuations about judgment and any coarse and repulsive pictures of blood and crucifixion and expiation for sin. Do not turn the cross into a slaughterhouse and the Gospel into a theology of the shambles. God is too good a being to have anything to do with such unpleasant things. All evil is from the other source and God is only good, only love, only blessing. A Saviour crucified for sinful man, that He might bear their curse and deliver them from the judgment due to them on account of their guilt and transgressions, a real atonement for sin by the vicarious death of an innocent Man for a guilty race? No, no, this is all repugnant to New Thought and the good-natured God our modern preachers have made out of the putty of their sentimental brains.

Alas for their wretched handiwork! One breath from the Spirit of truth will dissolve it as quickly as the thaw dissolves the splendid palace of ice in Montreal.

Come with me again and take another look at God's ancient picture gallery of the cross, and look at that awful object lesson, the Hebrew sin offering. What means this strange sight? I see a sinful man entering with trembling steps that sacred court. He is bowed down with the weight of conscious sin, perhaps his hand is stained with blood, at least his heart is heavy with the load of a guilty conscience. Ah, friends, it will take more than modern thought to annihilate that tremendous fact which history, poetry and drama have made part of the very fibre of human life, a guilty conscience, a sense of sin. Ask Lady Macbeth, the most tragic figure of dramatic art, why she cannot wipe out the foul stains of her horrid crime? Ask John Randolph of Roanoke what he meant by his dying cry, "Remorse, remorse, remorse!" Ask David why he wailed, "My sin is ever before me." Ask Judas if he has changed after two thousand years the awful confession with which he leaped to the abyss of woe, "I have sinned in that I have betrayed innocent blood." Ask the human heart in every age and every land if there is not something here called conscience, which sophistry cannot stifle and which even on earth oft becomes the worm that dieth not and the fire that is not quenched.

And so this poor sinner comes laden with his guilt to the altar of God, and he is leading by his side a lamb, a gentle, spotless, innocent lamb. Suddenly he pauses, and at the command of the ministering priest, he kneels and lays his hands solemnly upon the head of the lamb and confesses over it his sin. Instantly something strange and awful comes to pass. In the sight of the law and of God, his sin passes from him and is transferred to that innocent victim; and it becomes, as it were, a guilty thing, a mass of wickedness, a black and crimson curse that is no longer fit to live and that even dead is not fit to be offered in sacrifice upon the holy altar of God. Quickly its helpless life is taken from it, and as it lies bleeding, gasping and dying in agony, the sinful man beside it sees in its anguish the judgment which he deserved for his own transgressions. Its blood is quickly shed and sprinkled before the Lord as the offering up of its life instead of his. But its body, what shall we do with that? Offer it on God's altar? No! The lightnings of heaven would smite the hand that dared such a sacrilege. That body is an accursed thing, a mass of sin. Quickly it is hurried from the sacred precincts of the sanctuary of God. Away with it from this holy place. Outside the camp it is quickly burned and cast out to where the refuse and filth of the city is daily flung. Then that body is exposed and cut open, the entrails and the flesh forming together a ghastly and gory spectacle of hideous uncleanness—God's picture of the awfulness of sin; and then the whole mass is flung into the flames that are ever burning outside the camp, consuming such foul refuse and representing by their awful name, Gehenna, the fires of hell, for that word Gehenna is just the Hebrew name for hell.

Look at it long and well, that ancient picture of the Hebrew sin offering, and remember that it is God's last picture of the cross of Calvary, the death of Jesus Christ and the price of human redemption. Look at it and listen to these tremendous words: "He hath made to be sin for us who knew no sin, that we might be made the righteousness of God in Him." "Christ hath redeemed us from the curse of the law, being made a curse for us, for it is written, Cursed is every one that hangeth on a tree."

That is the doom which sin deserves, that is the doom which every sinner that rejects Jesus Christ must yet receive, exposed in all the aggravation of his guilt before the universe and then cast into the lake of fire. That is the hell Christ bore for you and me. Oh, sinful man, have you accepted His sacrifice or are you going to dare to meet your sin yourself? Come with all your guilt and lay your hands upon the head of the Lamb of God and cry,

> My faith would lay her hand
> On that dear head of Thine,
> While like a penitent I stand,
> And there confess my sin.

> Believing I rejoice
> To see the curse removed,
> I bless the Lamb with cheerful voice
> And sing His dying love.

I was called one night to see a colored woman who was dying close by where we were holding a tent meeting. Entering the room and kneeling by her bedside, I quoted to her awhile about Christ and then learned from her lip that she had been a terrible sinner, living a life of shame herself and dragging others down with her. At first she could scarcely believe that Christ would save such a sinner as she, but I told her about the Lamb of God and begged her to lay her hand upon His head and just roll over on Him all her burdens of sin. The vivid picture seemed to appeal to the strong imagination which is peculiar to this race, and after awhile she reached out her hand as though to put it on some invisible head. Then she began to confess and confess and confess until it seemed as if she would never end. She went over her sinful life, year after year, telling it all out as though I were not there, rolling the burden over on Jesus as though it was an infinite relief. As she rolled it out, her bosom heaved and sighed like the rolling of the sea and her voice rose and fell in strange cadences of agony and comfort. Several times I tried to stop her and finish with a word of prayer, for my meeting was waiting for me, but "no," she said, "hold on, I am not through yet." And so I let the meeting go while a burdened soul unloaded its burden at the cross. It must have been more than an hour before she seemed at last to be emptied of her awful load and began to shout her gratitude and thanks to the Saviour that had taken it all away. As we softly sang "There is a fountain filled with blood," it did really seem as though a white and spotless Lamb was standing by that bed and a black hand was passing over to Him a still blacker stream of lifelong sin and then as though

The Offering For Sin

that precious blood had washed it all away and that once guilty woman was whiter than the driven snow.

Oh, sinner, will you come and thus exchange your sin for His righteousness? For "He made sin for us who knew no sin that we might be made the righteousness of God in Him."

Dr. Clark tells in his journal of missionary travel how once in Africa he listened in a humble tent to the song of a lot of coolies who had been a band of cutthroats and murderers who had been marvelously redeemed. One of them, named Kothabye, had been the chief of a robber band and at last had been captured and sold as a slave. But no master would keep him, he was so wicked. At last a missionary bought him with the hope of saving him. One day he heard the missionary tell how the blood of Christ could cleanse a sinner. At the close he came up and in a stealthy voice asked, "Could he cleanse a murderer?"

"Yes," said the missionary.

"But if he had killed five men?"

"Yes," said the missionary, "the blood of Jesus Christ cleanseth from all sin."

"But if he had killed ten men?"

"Yes," said the missionary, "all manner of sin shall be forgiven unto men."

"But if he had killed twenty men?" "Yes," said the missionary, "though your sins be as scarlet, they shall be white as snow."

"But if he had killed thirty men?"

"Though they be red like crimson, they shall be as wool," answered the missionary.

"Then," said he, "I am that sinner, for I have killed thirty men." But the blood of Jesus Christ saved even that man, and he was now the leader of a coolie band of soul winners, and they were singing every night the song of thirty murders and the blood that could wash them all away.

Ah, but perhaps you have no such record and no deep sense of sin. Listen, the sin offering was for sins of ignorance especially, and the very condition of guilt was this, "Though he wist it not, yet he is guilty." God knows that down in the human heart there is a capacity for sin of which the sinner himself has never dreamed. God sees all that and it was for that that Jesus died. Do not wait till God lets you work it all out in your life as He has let some other sinners. The story is told of a painter who wanted a model for a painting of John on Patmos, and he found a beautiful young man and had him sit for the ideal portrait. Many years later he wanted to paint Judas Iscariot, and he looked through the prisons of Italy for a model that would fitly represent the worst of men. At last he found one and paid him to sit for the portrait. After he had finished he asked his name and history and found that it was the same young man who fifteen years before had represented the apostle of love. Such havoc had sin wrought in one short life! Oh, man and woman, you little know your future if you reject Jesus and God leaves you to yourself. For all the sin you know and for all the sin you do not know, Christ waits this moment to save and take it all away. If you have never committed any other great sin, greater than any sin you could have done is this sin of sins, the sin of rejecting Jesus and neglecting His great salvation. Tell me the secret of the unparalleled judgments that have fallen upon the Hebrew people for two thousand years. Was there ever a nation so scattered, peeled and crushed with the cruelty of men and the curse of heaven, and why? Listen, "His blood be upon us and our children." They sinned against the blood of Jesus; that is what you are doing. And for that, unless you turn from it to Him, there is no forgiveness. But even for that He waits to forgive and save. Will you come?

CHAPTER IV

SIN AND SALVATION

"Blessed is he whose transgression is forgiven, whose sin is covered. Blessed is the man unto whom the Lord imputeth not iniquity, and in whose spirit there is no guile"
(Psalm 32:1–2).

WE read in the introduction to this psalm, "A psalm of David, Maschil." The word "Maschil" is a Hebrew word which means "instruction." This is a psalm of instruction. It is not an appeal to our emotions but is a psalm presenting to us great truths about the things that concern our spiritual welfare. We will find instruction here first about sin; second about salvation; third about the means of salvation, repentance and confession; fourth about trouble and comfort in trouble; and finally about guidance in the practical life of every day. It is a unique psalm, and we shall trust the Lord to crowd in to a little while all this mass of deeply spiritual and most practical instruction covering every side of our life. Let us pray that some reader may pass on from sin to salvation and all the blessings that follow.

I. INSTRUCTION ABOUT SIN

I do not know any place where there is more instruction in a very few words about the nature, phases and far-reaching poison of sin. It is called by a number of names that are all characteristic and have distinct meanings that provide helpful teaching for us.

1. It is called *transgression*. "Blessed is he whose transgression is forgiven." The idea here suggested is the breaking of the law. Sin as a transgression of God's commandment. That is the most obvious form of wrongdoing. It refers to our acts, to the real things that we have done that we ought not to have done and the things we did not do which we ought to have done. God has a law, and that law is founded upon righteousness. It is necessary for the proper government of the universe. Human laws are essential. Without them there could be no peace or safety to the individual or community, and the kindest and most benevolent heart rejoices that there is a strong well-doer. Sin is the breaking up of this beneficent condition which God has established, and of which we have the image in our imperfect administration.

2. The next word is *sin*. "Blessed is he . . . whose sin is covered." Here there is something entirely different in the idea. The word for sin both in the Hebrew and Greek means to miss the mark, to miss the point at which we should have aimed. It is a coming short. It is a stepping aside from the thing which was best for us, missing our true aim and purpose in life and our real destiny. That is what sin is. It hurts us, it turns us aside, it perverts our way. It prevents God from doing for us what He was disposed to do and would have done if we ourselves had not hindered it. "The way of transgressors is hard." "He that sinneth against Me wrongeth his own soul." "All they that hate Me love death."

Sin And Salvation

Our shortcomings, our failures, our omissions are sin in this sense, and God looks with compassion upon sinners for this reason; they cannot hurt Him on His lofty throne, they are only harming themselves. There never was a more pathetic expression from the lips of our Saviour than His words about Zacchaeus the publican, "The Son of man is come to seek and to save that which is lost." This man that you despise, execrate and curse is just lost. I see him as a man that has missed his way and is on the wrong track, perverted the best things in his nature and turned then in the wrong direction. The lost man, the lost sheep, the lost coin, the lost child—that is God's deepest thought about sin, that it misses the mark, shuts us off from heaven and happiness, and perverts our whole nature.

3. The third word for sin is *iniquity*. "Blessed is the man unto whom the Lord imputeth not iniquity." The preposition "in," which prefixes the word, suggests that it refers primarily to inward, internal, intrinsic conditions. This word describes sin as it destroys our purity, perverts our nature, corrupts our heart and fills us with all the elements of wretchedness, misery and moral impotence. It is not the exhalations that rise from that marsh spreading malaria and poison, but it is the deep source of miasma from beneath from which poison and death will still continue to come until that marsh is drained and the poison destroyed. So the things you say and the things you do are of little account compared with that wrong nature, that wrong heart, that helpless spirit which will still keep on continuing in sin until the heart is regenerated and the heart sanctified.

4. "Blessed is the man ... in whose spirit there is no guile." *Guile* means falseness, the lack of truth or straightforwardness, a nature that is twisted and naturally perverted. There are sinners and great sinners that have sunk deep into evil, but

whom it is easy to save because they are honest sinners. They will see their evildoing, they will confess their wrong, they are willing to be helped and purified and saved. But there are others who would evade and deceive themselves and who will return again to their evildoing by a naturally perverted and crooked nature. Guile is the worst thing in human depravity, the lack of honesty, the lack of a right purpose and of a true will and real desire to be saved from sin. Willing to be saved from hell, willing to be saved from disgrace, willing to be delivered from the consequences they have brought upon themselves, yet they cling to their old sinful ways. That is what Jeremiah cried in utter despair of ruined human nature, "The heart is deceitful above all things." It is not honest. It doesn't really want to be right. It is "deceitful above all things," and, therefore, "desperately wicked: who can know it?" There is no hope for the man who is not straightforward, who is not honest, upright, sincere, not willing to stand in the light and have God help him. There is God's picture of sin. Isn't it an awful picture and isn't it a true one?

II. INSTRUCTION ABOUT SALVATION

Here again we have four sides to it.

1. *Forgiveness.* "Blessed is he whose transgression is forgiven." The idea here is the lifting of a burden. That is the original sense of the Hebrew word: relieving the burdened heart of its sense of guilt, its fear of punishment.

Poor Christian, groaning under his load in "Pilgrim's Progress," until at last as he came to the place called Calvary. The string began to crack, and the burden rolled away and sank into the empty grave of Jesus. Forgiveness is that which you perhaps cannot explain as a theologian; you haven't yet learned how or why God can so forgive you, but you have come with your heavy load, laid it at His feet and asked forgiveness in the name of Jesus. Your burden has rolled away, your heart is filled with joy and praise, and your response is "I will praise Thee, for Thou wast angry with me, but Thine anger is turned away."

2. *Expiation.* "Blessed is the man whose sins are covered." This refers to the atoning work of the Lord Jesus Christ, His precious blood and righteousness, covering the sin from the sight of a holy God so that He can say, "I have not seen iniquity in Jacob nor perverseness in Israel." Plenty to see, but it is covered. God does not see it anymore. Like the snow that falls upon the backyard and the dust and refuse are all covered, so God says, "Though your sins be as scarlet, they shall be as white as snow." They are covered. You have done nothing to make yourself worthy, but God has covered them out of sight through some other means apart altogether from your making. God goes further before He gets through. He not only covers them, but He destroys them, but we have not reached that yet.

In the old tabernacle there was a very striking picture. Up in the Holy of Holies was the Shekinah, the eye of God, a blazing glory that looked down into the ark beneath it representing God's eye looking upon the record within that ark. What was the record? A broken law. The law was there, that law had just been broken, had been shattered by Moses on the Mount, broken to fragments as an emblem of the fact that man and the people had broken all this law actually. What was the use of keeping the tablets intact when the principles had been dishonored? The law was a broken law and God's holy eye was looking down upon that broken law; and if He had continued to see it He could have had no fellowship with those people. He could only have dealt with them in judgment. What did He do? He ordered that a covering should be put over the ark—a Mercy Seat. It was covered with blood. It was closed down over the broken law, and as the eye of God looked down, it did not see the broken law but the covering of blood. The worshipper could sing, "Blessed is the man whose sin is covered and to whom the Lord doth not impute iniquity." Sin was covered through the atonement of Jesus, through His death in your stead, through His taking upon Him your guilt and being treated as you deserved to be treated until it was finished and He had made an end of sin and He had borne all that you deserved to bear and through His substitutionary work you are saved. God cannot forgive sin without satisfaction. He must deal with it. He did deal with it in Jesus Christ, and every man or woman united to Jesus Christ gets the benefit of His atonement.

That is why the Publican prayed, "God be merciful to me the sinner," not, "God, overlook my sin because You are so merciful." That is what the Unitarian tells you, that is what the New Theology tells you: God is so good and kind He will overlook it without any settling. This Publican did not say that. The word in the original is, "God be the propitiation (the old word for bloody covering) for me, the sinner," and it is the same old faith in the blood of Jesus that you and I exercise when we are saved.

I remember a man once saying to me, after I had been preaching on the parable of the prodigal son, "I was delighted to hear you preach about the parable of the lost son last Sunday night. That is just what I believe. I see no need for any other Gospel than the Fatherhood of God, that great Heart that is just ready without any consideration to take back His child."

But I said, "My brother, please wait until next Sunday night. I am going to preach on the Good Shepherd. The parable of the prodigal son doesn't stand alone; it stands with two other parables. The Father could not have taken back his boy if the Shepherd had not gone in the other parable and prepared the way. He is the Shepherd, the bleeding Christ, the suffering Lamb of God, the One that went far into the wilderness and mountains and night to save that which was lost, and it is because we have the Good Shepherd that we have the father of the prodigal." Stand by this Gospel, beloved, if you expect God to stand by you, the sinner. Sin is covered. Are yours covered? Are you trusting only in that blood, dear friends, to stand between you and the holy eye of God?

3. The third word is one which we translate in our theology as *justification*. Here it is "imputeth not." "Blessed is the man unto whom the Lord imputeth not iniquity." The word "impute" means to have a thought against one. God does not think sin against you, does not cherish a grudge, does not remember it. It does not mean that you are worthy, but it means that God counts you worthy for the sake of somebody else. Saved on the merits of Jesus Christ. You are a sinner, but God doesn't hold it against you. He transfers the account to Jesus. Christ steps forward and says, "Put this man's sin to my account and accept him as you would accept Me." So we read, "He hath made us accepted in the Beloved," in the Son of His love. We cannot be loose in our idea about salvation. We must take the trouble to understand what God has taken the trouble to do and say and rest our hope for eternal life definitely and explicitly on the finished work of the Lord Jesus Christ. "Imputeth not" means that He forgets all about it: "I will remember your sins no more." I will treat you as though you had never sinned. When God saves us for the sake of Jesus, He puts us in as good a place as if we were Jesus, as if you were His own dear Son. He doesn't hold you off at arm's length and say, "You miserable sinner, I won't punish you just now, and if you behave yourself, I will save you," but He takes you in His arms and seats you in the heavenlies and talks

about you as if you were already there. He has forgotten all about it. If you went to God and talked about the things put under the blood five years ago, He would look astonished and say, "I don't understand you. Why those things have been annihilated. I forgave them, they are gone, you cannot bring them up without crucifying afresh the Son of God and putting Him to an open shame."

4. The word *guile* is met by the word *cleanse*. The guile is taken away, the crookedness is made straight and the heart is brought to the place where its will is yielded in complete surrender and its choice and thought is, "Not my will, O Lord, but Thine be done." That is holiness; that is the essence of purification, cleansing and the deeper spiritual life. It is to have a purpose that is true. It is to have a will that has chosen God unconditionally and eternally, and when you put yourself there by the grace of God, God is bound to give to you the fullness of His grace and bring you up to the place where you have chosen to stand through His grace.

III. THE MEANS OF SALVATION

They are conviction and repentance. We have it all here in this psalm. For a while he tells us he was impenitent. "When I kept silence my bones waxed old through my roaring all the day long. For day and night Thy hand was heavy upon me: my moisture is turned into the drought of summer." He refused to see his sin and lay asleep in the insensibility of an unconvicted conscience. Men can do that long. David was two years during which he never thought of the murder of Uriah or the wrong he had done his wife. It never once occurred to him. Ah, but there comes a time when God breaks the silence, breaks in upon your security, and the convicting Holy Ghost comes with the thunders of God's providence and the terrors of a guilty conscience and the accusation of Satan too. Blessed is the man that lets God speak to him even through the terrors of conviction and a guilty conscience. Don't silence that voice; it is your last friend. Don't tear that hand away that is gently laid upon your shoulder; it is God's angel hastening you out of Sodom before God's judgment falls. So the conviction comes and the Holy Ghost makes you unhappy. You cannot pray a better prayer for one who is wandering from God than that God will make them unhappy. Don't get frightened and think they are getting nervous prostration. Don't lightly heal the hurt of the daughter of my people. God has been answering prayer; let Him speak until they listen and answer.

Next comes confession. "I acknowledge my sin unto thee and my iniquity have I not hid." It doesn't mean that I felt very badly about it, that I made a great show of tears and that I promised that I would be good, that I turned over a new leaf and did my best to save myself. No, I stopped excusing myself and making it seem right and give some reason why I had been drawn into it. I called it as black as God called it. I said I was a sinner and stood out in the light of conscience and the Holy Ghost and said, "God be merciful to me, the sinner." "If we confess our sins, He is faithful and just to forgive us our sins and to cleanse us from all unrighteousness." But the sin must be acknowledged to God. You are not bound to tell the world the secrets of your heart and life; all you have to do with men is to make right the things that are wrong between you and them, but your secret soul must be open to God, and to Him you must tell everything, and honestly, and with absolute precision about it. You must call the thing what God calls it.

What beauty there is in the description here of God's mercy. I said, "I will confess my transgressions unto the Lord; and Thou forgavest the iniquity of my sin." I made up my mind to do it, and before I had time to do it, while I was beginning to do it,

God's mercy met me more than halfway, and "Thou forgavest." It is a great outburst of amazement and thanksgiving: "Thou forgavest the iniquity of my sin," not only my sin, but the dark intrinsic evil of it—took it all away. And He did it perhaps before I got halfway through. It reminds us of the prodigal who said, "I will arise and go to my father and say, Father, I have sinned against heaven, and before thee." Thus he made up his speech and finished with a business proposition: "I am no more worthy to be called thy son; make me as one of thy hired servants." He thought that was rather straight. He arose and went to his father, and when he was "a great way off, his father saw him and ran." It takes a great deal to make an old man run. But he ran, and faster than the boy, too, I am sure. And the boy had just time to say, "Father, I have sinned," and before he got any further, the father choked the rest of it out of him and he could not finish the sentence. He was forgiven before he got halfway through. The father did not allow him to say that speech about being a hired servant. He was a son. He knew it. That was what the psalmist said: "I said I will confess my transgressions," and the moment God saw he meant it, God was there with His everlasting arms and great heart of love. Oh, sinner, come, come to such a Father, to such a heart, to such loving arms of mercy; come honest, straight; tell Him all. You think it is going to kill you. He will meet you before you get there, and you will never have such luxury as that first moment of confessing sin unto the Lord.

IV. HELP IN TROUBLE

"Thou art my hiding place; Thou shalt preserve me from trouble; Thou shalt compass me about with songs of deliverance." There is time for only one thought here. Wasn't it a great mercy that he got saved before the trouble came? Suppose he had gone through that storm without God's mercy. What would have become of him? Ah, dear friend, it is because God knows trouble is coming to you that He wants to get you saved first so that you may go through leaning on the everlasting arms with no reproach from your conscience, and no ghastly shadows of your sinful life. Or, suppose that your last illness should come this week, suppose that sickness should strike you down and your brain should become wild with delirium and the devil bring the skeletons of the past and the visions of the future to pass before you unsaved, you would die of fear as much as of sickness. Lots of people are healed because they go through their sickness with a peaceful conscience. Beloved, the trouble is coming; it is coming surely. It may come soon, and it is because God knows it that He is pleading with you now. Perhaps He has been breaking up your life this past summer and fall and your bones have been waxing old through your roaring all the day long, and His hand has been heavy upon you, and everything has been going wrong in your life. It is because there is greater trouble ahead for you and the Lord wants you to be saved before it comes. He wants you to go into it saying, "Thou art my hiding place; Thou shalt preserve me from trouble; Thou shalt compass me about with songs of deliverance."

V. THERE IS STILL ANOTHER INSTRUCTION

Guidance for practical, everyday living: "I will instruct thee and teach thee in the way which thou shalt go; I will guide thee with Mine eye. Be ye not as the horse, or as the mule, which have no understanding; whose mouth must be held in with bit and bridle." God does not save us and leave us to trudge on our pilgrim way alone. He meets us at the gates of life and takes our hand and leads us all the way home. You say, I am afraid I won't stand. Of course not, if you go alone. He is going to stand with you. He is going to show you the way and enable you to take it.

What a beautiful picture we have here of His teaching. "I will instruct thee and teach thee in the way which thou shalt go." I'll not command you; I'll not send out a flaming law and say, If you don't keep it, I will destroy you. No, I will instruct thee and teach thee. *Instruct* means by slow degrees, line upon line, precept upon precept, here a little and there a little. He will teach you like a little child, and He will so instruct you that you shall understand and shall be taught in the way that you should go. Yes, He will so teach you that you will not need to be guided by a milepost along the road or by a written command or by a bridle or a bit in your mouth; but He will guide you with His eye. "I will guide thee with Mine eye." Surely that means I will give you such nearness to Me that you will catch My very thought, that you intuitively will know what I want you to do that you will have no difficulty about your way. I will put My eye inside of you. I will be your Eye, your Judgment, a law within; His thought in us, His mind in us so that we don't have to struggle to get light, but with a simple surrendered will, our light breaks forth as the morning and we get an intuition of the thing He would have us do. And He will guide you, beloved, with His eye. So He says, don't be as a horse or mule which has to be put in harness, or lest they come near thee, but rather if you would have them come near you. You can't get them near you to serve you unless you tie them by harness. That is a good way for horses, asses and mules, but a bad way for Christians to live. And yet many people will not turn from wrong until God has got to go at them with a club, let some calamity come, let something go wrong in their lives. Elihu tells how sometimes "God speaketh once, yea, twice, yet man perceived it not. In a dream, in a vision of the night, when deep sleep falleth upon men, in slumbering upon the bed; then he opened the ears of men, and sealeth their instruction, that He may withdraw man from his purpose, and hide pride from man. He is chastened also with pain, and the multitude of his bones with strong pain.

Lo, all these worketh God oftentimes with man, to bring back his soul from the pit, to be enlightened with the light of the living" (Job 33:14–17, 19, 29– 30). "All these things worketh God oftentimes with man." That is the bit and bridle. Don't compel God to do that with you. When we are judged, we are chastened of the Lord, but if we would judge ourselves we should not be judged. If you would only listen and see what God wants you to do, you would not be judged.

"Many sorrows shall be to the wicked." That is why they have so much trouble. God has to put the bridle on them. But "ye that are upright in heart," ye that have a single purpose to serve God, "be glad in the Lord, and rejoice, and shout for joy."

I looked, and lo! from Calvary's cross

A healing stream so pure

Engulfed my soul and now I sing

Praise God, I am secure.

CHAPTER V

REDEMPTION THROUGH HIS BLOOD

"He hath made us accepted in the Beloved. In whom we have redemption though His blood, the forgiveness of sins, according to the richness of His grace; Wherein he hath abounded toward us in all wisdom and prudence; in whom also we have obtained an inheritance, being predestinated according to the purpose of Him who worketh all things after the counsel of His own will; that we should be to the praise of His glory"
(Ephesians 1:6–8, 11–12).

IN the clear, logical order of thought in this great epistle, the writer punctuates the different paragraphs and marks the sequence of his lofty argument by closing each section with a kind of doxology. This is expressed by the phrase which appears so often in this chapter, "To the praise of the glory of His grace," or "to the praise of His glory."

Following this suggestion, the second great section of his review of the blessings of the Spirit commences in the middle of the sixth verse and leads to the discussion of the glorious blessing of our redemption through the blood of Christ and our acceptance, forgiveness and final and full salvation in Him.

The first step in pursuance of the divine purpose with which the epistle opens is redemption. This is described with great completeness and spiritual fervor. We have:

I. THE REDEEMER

"He hath made us accepted in the Beloved." Literally this reads "in the Son of His Love." The whole story of redemption is personal. It brings us at every step into direct contact with the Redeemer Himself. At the very outset He is presented to us in the most attractive, majestic and tender aspect as the "Son of His Love." The Father did not commit this mighty undertaking to any ordinary agent. He chose heaven's noblest, brightest, mightiest Being. The verse implies that He is the Son of God in the most exclusive and special sense. Elsewhere He is represented as His "only Begotten" and His "well beloved Son." His high and divine character gives the first assurance of His ability to carry out the supreme task with which He was entrusted. All the infinite resources of Deity were at His command. He had right of access to the Father under all circumstances, and His divine dignity gave to His personal work the value which no creative being could have claimed. One drop of His precious blood would have been sufficient to atone for the sins of the world.

But the special aspect under which He is presented here is that of nearness and dearness to the Father. He is the Son of His love. This assures us of the Father's intense and affectionate interest in the great work of redemption and the subjects who are to be benefited by that work. He puts their case in the hands of the One that is dearest to Him. It becomes bound up with the very life of His Beloved, and it is impossible, therefore, that it could in any way be neglected or allowed to fail.

It is said that once an Egyptian king was so concerned in the successful raising of a valuable obelisk that he fastened his only son, the heir to the throne, to the highest point of the obelisk, and then he said to his engineers: "The life of my son is bound up with the success of your work. Be careful what you do. The failure of your task means death to my child and profound responsibility for you." So God bound up the redemption of this world with His well-beloved Son, and all that is dear to Him is responsible for the successful accomplishment of this plan of infinite grace and love. He has put the life of Jesus into the scale with us, and together they are to weigh all possible difficulties, hindrance or questions of cost.

But, again, this beautiful description of the Redeemer implies also a nearness and dearness of the place into which we are brought through our connection with Him. Accepted in the Son of His Love we become like Him, the children of His love, as dear as He. Identified with His person and with His name, clothed with His righteousness, covered with His blood, we can sing:

> So dear, so very dear to God,
>
> Dearer I cannot be;
>
> For in the person of His Son,
>
> I am as dear as He.

II. THE REDEMPTION

"In whom we have redemption through His blood." Redemption means deliverance through a ransom, release from a claim and the judgment through a settlement of the claim. It is not mere good will and clemency overlooking a fault and blotting out a record, but it is strict justice recognizing the claim to its fullest extent, meeting every liability and giving the receipt in full through the substitution of another's worth and kindness. There is a milk and water type of sentimental theology widely prevalent, and wandering from the truth perhaps through a morbid straining after originality and philosophical speculation, which would make us believe that the cross of Jesus Christ was just an object lesson on the part of God to show to the world the beauty of patience, submission, self-sacrifice, and the passive virtues so sublimely exhibited in the character of Jesus. They are willing to admit also that it was a striking exhibition of God's love fitted to attract and melt the hearts of men; but it was for stage effect, and back of it there was no essential necessity for any vicarious suffering. There was no question of law or expiation or the substitution of an innocent for a guilty person. In a word, there is no real atonement by blood, but it is all designed for moral impression and spiritual persuasion. This is not the Bible's doctrine of redemption. This is "another gospel," of which the apostle Paul has said, whosoever shall preach it "let him be accursed."

Redemption by the blood recognizes, in the first place, the real fact of sin, and the inexorable necessity of satisfying the claims of justice, equity and law. There is something in the instincts of humanity which is part of the fitness of things, and a direct intuition from the Creator Himself which tells us that to lightly overlook wrong is in itself the grossest wrong. The man who can think with cold blood and unmoved spirit of the Armenian outrages, the Cuban wrongs, the shameful outrage of innocence, helplessness and virtue is himself destitute of a true moral sense, and capable, perhaps, of doing these very things. Should it appear that the national calamity which a few days ago hurled hundreds of helpless seamen into eternity was an act of premeditated design, the instinct of common humanity would demand satisfaction, and the man whose heart did not respond to this instinct would be recognized as a monster. It is not the cry for revenge. It may be accompanied with a generous forgiveness, but there must be a due recognition of the fact of wrong, or all the principles of righteousness and government are disintegrated and the universe is a chaos.

The old heroic Roman but gave voice to this sentiment when his own son was brought before him with treasonable crime, and the law and the testimony both demanded his death. A thousand voices pleaded for his life from family, from state, from the father's own heart, but he sternly answered: "I am a father, and have my human feelings as truly as you; but I am a judge, and I must be just."

This is part of the constitution of nature and the very character of God, and therefore He could not overlook sin without ceasing to be God. His fatherly heart prompted the love that would save the guilty, but His perfect attributes demanded the settlement of the question of eternal righteousness. It was then that His wisdom devised the wondrous plan that the Son of His love should come and take upon Himself the nature and the responsibility of the sinful race, and should be punished in their stead and settle in their behalf every question and every claim, and then that they on His account should be dealt with on the ground of His settlement and released through the ransom that He had paid.

Blood, which is here described as the ransom, just means life: "The life is in the blood; therefore have I given the blood as an atonement." Our life had been forfeited, He gave His life instead, and then through His divine power He received back a new life and He gives us this resurrection life as ours. Thus His life was given for us first, and now it is given to us. This is the Scriptural doctrine of the atonement. It runs like a crimson thread through every ancient sacrifice and type. We see it in the scapegoat on which the priest confessed the sins of the people, and then sent it out into the lone wilderness to die in agony and as an accursed thing. We see it in the sin offering. The spotless lamb on whose head the sinner lay his hands and confessed his sin until that innocent victim became in the eye of the law a mass of horrid wickedness, and was carried outside the camp, flayed, laid open in ghastly gore and held upon the consuming flame as a spectacle of judgment. So "He was made sin for us who knew no sin, that we might be made the righteousness of God in Him."

Now we do not come cringing and begging for mercy as a capricious favor, but our blessed Advocate stands with us at court, presents the full atonement for every claim, offers a receipt in full written in His own blood, and demands from the Judge a verdict in our favor and full victory, nay, a public justification, and sends us forth without a spot or stain upon our record looking in the face of Satan and the universe crying, "Who is He that condemneth? It is Christ that died. Who shall lay anything to the charge of God's elect?"

This, we believe, was the meaning of that sublime scene described in the Apocalypse. When Jesus Christ entered heaven after His triumphant resurrection, presented the settlement in full of all demands for His redeemed people, the order went forth that Satan, the accuser of the brethren, should be expelled from the court of heaven and never allowed to lift his voice against us again, and as the angels drove him forth with their fiery swords, the shout went up, "Rejoice, ye heavens, for the accuser of our brethren is cast down, that accused them day and night before God."

Beloved, this is redemption. Can you say with humble and yet triumphant faith, "In whom we have redemption through His blood"?

III. FORGIVENESS

"Forgiveness of sins according to the riches of His grace." Forgiveness is not the same as redemption. It is the effect of redemption. Redemption is the settlement of the claim. Forgiveness is the receipt handed to us and shaking hands over the adjustment. Redemption is the paying off of the mortgage. Forgiveness is the "satisfaction piece," which is handed over after the release. Forgiveness is not a mere feeling of peace or effort. It is the simple fact accepted by faith on the ground of completed redemption. It does not depend upon your good feelings or even the promise of your good behavior, but it rests entirely upon the finished atonement of Jesus and is claimed according to His word by simple trust. Therefore, we read, "If we confess our sins, He is faithful and just to forgive us our sins." His mercy and love are not even appealed to here. But it is His faithfulness and justice that are represented as demanding our forgiveness. His faithfulness simply means that He keeps His Word, and His justice means that He does that which is right. Now, if God did not forgive us when we came claiming it on the ground of Christ's redemption, He would be a liar, and he that believeth not hath made Him a liar. If it were possible for you to go down to the depths of hell and proclaim throughout eternity, "I came to Christ as He invited me and He cast me out," your testimony would do God more harm than all the devil ever did or said. God can never afford to have a soul say, "He refused to forgive me when I came and took Him at His Word." He is faithful to forgive and He is just to forgive. Now there isn't a man or woman in the world who makes the faintest claim to honesty who would dare to take two prices for the same article. If your customer shows you a receipt proving that he has paid for it once, you would be a scoundrel if you demanded he should pay for it again. Now, if Christ has paid for our salvation and the price has been accepted by God, it would simply be dishonesty for God to make us pay the debt again. It is therefore a simple matter of justice for God to forgive us our sins. So He says to us, "I have blotted out as a thick cloud your transgressions and as a cloud your sins." "Put Me in remembrance, let us plead together; declare thou, that thou mayest be justified." He wants you to bring your arguments, to plead His promises, to claim your redemption rights, and to take your place by faith as a sinner and then claim the sinner's Saviour. Oh, how strong a consolation He has given us, "who have fled for refuge to the hope set before us."

Beloved, have you received forgiveness through the blood by redemption, and are you rejoicing in the glad testimony, "I will praise Thee, you Thou wast angry with me, but thine anger is turned away and Thou comfortest me"?

IV. THE RICHES OF HIS GRACE

Not only is it forgiveness, but "abundant forgiveness," according to the riches of His grace "wherein He hath abounded toward us in all wisdom and prudence." How abundant His forgiving love! Listen to His description of His mercy. He says He will cast our sins into the depths of the sea. He will cast them behind His back. He will remember them no more. As a thick cloud, He has blotted them out. As far as the East from the West (and they never meet), so far hath He removed our transgressions from us.

He tells us in this passage that "He hath abounded toward us in all wisdom and prudence." This might be translated foresight. He has looked forward to our failures and our faults. He has foreseen every one of them. When He took us, first He knew all that we would do and fail to do. Nay, when He chose us in the eternal ages, He fortified Himself even against our unworthiness. He is ready for every emergency. This should not make us presume to sin, for if we continue to do this willfully, we do not belong to Him. But it should give us encouragement and comfort. At the same time, the language here throws a fine light on God's disciplinary dealings with us even when He forgives us.

He does it with all wisdom and prudence. He sometimes keeps back from us for a time the comfort and the joy for which we are seeking, and makes us feel the keen pain of sin, not because He is angry, but because He is lovingly making us understand how exceedingly bitter and evil a thing sin is, and He is putting the bitter herbs of a heavenly discipline along with the blood of the Passover and the assurance of His mercy and His grace. Let us take His mercy under all circumstances, and let us, at the same time, trust His wisdom and His heavenly love.

V. THE RICHES OF HIS GLORY

The lofty flight of the apostle's argument does not end until it reaches a still higher region. In the last theme, he began way back in the eternal past. He carries us on here to the eternal future. He gives us in a series of bold and almost mysterious senses a lofty vision of the ages to come, when all the outcome of this redemption shall be disclosed, and when our full inheritance shall be completely realized and we shall know Him, the light and the glory of the ages to come, how much redemption cost and how much it brought us.

First, he tells us that in the fullness of time, Christ is to gather together into one all things in heaven and in earth. He is not merely undoing the calamity of the fall, but He is working out a sublime consummation for which the worlds were made. He is preparing an empire of unutterable glory in which He and His redeemed bride share the throne and shall be the centre of the whole economy of God. It shall be a consummation in which everything glorious in heaven and everything dear and beautiful on earth shall have part. It shall be the combination of all history and all creation in a glorious new creation. It shall be all that is best and brightest and sweetest and gladdest from every part of the universe of God brought together in one eternal paragon of beauty and of blessing. Everything shall be in harmony. There shall be no discords. He is to gather everything into one. We shall have no uncongenial surroundings. We shall be in harmony with ourselves. We shall be in harmony with others. We shall be in harmony with our surroundings, and Christ shall be the centre and crown, the joy of all.

Now, he tells us that we have obtained an inheritance in this glorious consummation. It was for that He chose us ages ago. It was for that He redeemed us. It is for that He saves us. It is for that we have let go of all other heritages of selfishness, earthliness and the forbidden world of sense and sin. Oh, beloved, have you made your eternal inheritance secure?

But there is a fine term in this verse. Rotherham translates it, "In whom we are taken as an inheritance." Not only have we an inheritance, but we are His inheritance. For us He has let go of all other honors, glories, joys and taken us to be His portion, "For the Lord's portion is His people, and Jacob is the lot of His inheritance." What is He going to get out of us? Shall we let Him refine, educate and glorify us until we shall meet His own ideal and reach His glorious likeness? He shall have the ineffable joy of presenting us to Himself a "glorious bride, not having spot or wrinkle or any such thing," and in this consummation He shall see of the travail of His soul and be satisfied," and we "shall be satisfied when we awake in His likeness."

Beloved, we are standing between two mighty eternities. We have just looked back to the ages past and seen in the dim distance the moment when we were chosen in Him, and we have attempted to look into the radiant glory in the remote future and catch a glimpse of what it will be when, in the ages to come, His mighty purpose shall be fulfilled. Oh, let these two infinite outlooks inspire us, enlarge us and lift us up into the high and holy dignity of sons of God and heirs of glory, and send us forth to walk henceforth worthy of the vocation wherewith we are called.

CHAPTER VI

BACK TO CALVARY

"The preaching of the cross is to them that perish foolishness" (1 Corinthians 1:18).

"God forbid that I should glory, save in the cross of our Lord Jesus Christ" (Galatians 6:14).

FOOLISHNESS. This is the world's estimate of the cross of Christ, the estimate of the cultured Grecian of the first century and the philosopher of the twentieth century. Christ, a lofty example, a heroic sufferer, a noble martyr for a worthy cause, a pattern of self-sacrificing love; yes, if you please, the noblest character of history and the loftiest example of the altruism of the ages.

But Christ, a sacrifice for sin, a substitute for sinners, a ransom for lost men; no, never. This is the theology of the shambles; this is a relic of pagan superstitions; this is impossible for modern ideas of reason, justice and humanity, and some even dare to say the blood of Christ means no more than the blood of some heroic fireman or sailor who anywhere sacrifices his life for the rescue of his perishing fellow being.

In sublime contrast with the wisdom of the world and the pride of reason, we hear the great apostle proclaiming, "God forbid that I should glory save in the cross of our Lord Jesus Christ." And as we listen, we hear the echo rolling back from the choruses of the ransomed and the songs of the seraphim, "Blessing and honor, and glory and power be unto Him that sitteth upon the throne and unto the Lamb forever and ever. Worthy is the Lamb that was slain to receive power and riches and wisdom and strength and honor and glory and blessing."

Back to Calvary! Let us glance first at the witnesses and then at their testimony.

I. THE WITNESSES

1. Nature itself is a witness for the cross. The Lord Jesus appealed to it in introducing His sublime address on the cross in John 12:24–26: "Except a corn of wheat fall into the ground and die, it abideth alone; but if it die it bringeth forth much fruit. He that loveth his life shall lose it; and he that hateth his life in this world shall keep it unto life eternal. If any man serve Me let him follow Me."

The law of death and resurrection is fundamental in the natural world. The seed must perish before the harvest comes. The coral builder rears the great Pacific Islands through its own death over its sepulchre. The mother bird will gladly give her life to save her young. Everywhere it is true,

> "Life evermore is fed by death
>
> In earth and sea and sky,
>
> And that a rose may breathe its breath
>
> Something must die."

The cross of Jesus Christ, therefore, is in harmony with the great principle which underlies the divine creation. It has yet to stamp its impress on the heavens and earth, which themselves shall pass away, and give place to the new creation when He that sitteth upon the throne shall say: "Behold, I make all things new."

2. The instincts and traditions of human nature all point to the principle of vicarious suffering in expiation of sin. We see this in the crudest as well as the most intelligent of the world's faiths. The Hindus have a striking legend of the god Vishnu being once appealed to by a human soul that was pursued by a serpent. Vishnu changed the soul into a dove which flew up above the serpent's reach. But immediately the serpent became transformed into a hawk which pursued the dove until in terror it appealed again to Vishnu, who opened his bosom and gave the trembling dove a place of refuge in his heart. Then the hawk demanded that Vishnu should give back some indemnity for the loss of its prey, and it was willing to be satisfied with an equal portion of the living flesh and blood of Vishnu's breast. The god bared his bosom and the hawk tore from his breast an equal portion of the quivering flesh until he was satisfied. In this and countless other shadows of human tradition, we find continual foregleams pointing to Calvary, and although all these are unworthy of the sublime spectacle afforded by redeeming love, yet they show how the principle of vicarious suffering is innate in the human conscience.

3. The promises and prophecies of Scripture all point to Calvary. The germ of Messianic prophecy appears in the first revelation of grace in Eden, that the seed of the woman should bruise the serpent's head, but the serpent should bruise his heel. The conflict thus foreshadowed reappears through all the prophetic messages and reaches its climax in the fifty-third chapter of Isaiah in the crimson picture of the Man of Sorrows who was wounded for our

transgressions, bruised for our iniquities and by whose stripes we are healed.

Our Lord in His conversation with His disciples on the way to Emmaus refers to this prophetic foreshadowing of the cross in the plainest terms: "Thus it is written, and thus it behooved Christ to suffer, and to rise from the dead on the third day. Ought not Christ to have suffered these things, and to enter into His glory?"

4. The types of the Old Testament, in vivid, symbolic language, all point to Calvary. The coats of skins, with which God clothed our guilty parents, Adam and Eve, were clearly significant of the blood and righteousness of the coming Saviour. Abel's bleeding offering brought him acceptance, while Cain's more attractive fruits and flowers were rejected. The smoke of Noah's altar brought from heaven the covenant promise that the earth should never again be submerged by flood. The sacrifice of Isaac on Mount Moriah was eloquent of the cross. The sprinkled blood of the Paschal lamb was an eloquent symbol of the redeeming blood. The two little birds employed in the cleansing of the leper set forth the death and resurrection of Jesus Christ. The ghastly horrors of the sin offering and the sweet-smelling savor of the burnt offering and the beautiful spectacle of the scapegoat bearing the sins of the people into the desolation of the wilderness. All these provided but one message, and it pointed straight to Calvary and proclaimed, "Behold the Lamb of God." The Jewish tabernacle was the most complete and perfect foreshadowing of the coming redemption. Every portion of its furniture and every rite of its imposing ceremonial echoed the one significant truth, "Without the shedding of blood there is no remission of sin."

The story of many of the characters of the Old Testament is suggestive of vicarious suffering. Joseph suffered innocently through the sins of his brethren, and thus became their saviour.

Moses was the constant victim of their gainsaying and rebellion. Jeremiah could say in language that prefigured Christ, "Behold, and see if there be any sorrow like unto my sorrow." Jonah's experience is quoted by Christ Himself as a distinct type of His death and resurrection.

5. John the Baptist, the forerunner, was sent for the express purpose of identifying and introducing the Messiah. It is not a little remarkable that the very first impression of John on meeting the modest prophet of Nazareth was that which all the types had so vividly foreshadowed, His sacrificial suffering and death. "Behold," he cries, not the prophet, the Messiah, the King of Israel, but "Behold the Lamb of God which taketh away the sin of the world." It is thus that he introduces Him to Israel. It is thus that he recognizes Him as the Great High Priest and the vicarious victim of the cross of Calvary. If we accept the testimony of John at all, we must recognize the Lord Jesus Christ above all else as our crucified and suffering Redeemer and the great Sin Bearer of the world.

6. Our Lord Himself bears witness to the cross again and again as the goal of His first advent. "The Son of man came not to be ministered unto, but to minister and to give His life a ransom for many," was His answer to the fleshly ambition of His own disciples. "This cup is the New Testament in My blood which is shed for many for the remission of sins," is His own explanation of the most sacred of His ordinances for keeping alive His memory to the end of time. "As Moses lifted up the serpent in the wilderness, even so must the Son of man be lifted up," was His first message of the Gospel in Jerusalem. And later He repeats the same significant phrase,

"I, if I be lifted up from the earth, will draw all men unto Me." And the evangelist adds the impressive note, "This He said signifying what death He should die." There was no illusion in the Master's heart about the closing drama of His earthly life, and when one of His disciples presumed to call in question such an idea as that He should be crucified, He turned upon him in holy indignation and declared, "Get thee behind Me, Satan." And this is still His attitude toward all who dishonor or ignore His precious blood.

7. The testimony of the Apostles and writers of the New Testament is a fitting climax to all this cloud of witnesses. We ask Peter, and he answers, "Ye were not redeemed with corruptible things, such as silver and gold, but with the precious blood of Christ." "Christ was once offered the just for the unjust that He might bring us to God." "Who His own self bare our sins in His own body to the tree." "Inasmuch, then, as Christ hath suffered for us in the flesh, arm yourselves likewise with the same mind." We ask John, and he replies, "He is the propitiation for our sins, and not for ours only, but also for the sins of the whole world." "The blood of Jesus Christ, His Son, cleanseth us from all sin." "Unto Him that loved us and washed us from our sin in His own blood, unto Him be glory and dominion forever and ever, amen." And Paul brings up the train with his repeated testimony, "Whom God hath set forth to be the propitiation through faith in His blood, in whom we have redemption through His blood, even the forgiveness of sins, according to the riches of His grace." "I declare unto you the gospel, how that Christ died for our sins according to the Scriptures." "We thus judge that if one died for all, then all died," "God was in Christ, reconciling the world unto Himself, not imputing their trespasses unto them." And when

all languages fail, we have the power of expression by the apostrophe of our text, "God forbid that I should glory, save in the cross of our Lord Jesus Christ."

These are the witnesses, and their testimony is echoed by sixty generations of ransomed men in earth and heaven, who seem to say,

> "Dear dying Lamb, Thy precious blood
> Shall never lose its power,
> Till all the ransomed church of God
> Be saved to sin no more"

II. THEIR TESTIMONY

No subject has been more widely or variously discussed than the atonement of our Lord Jesus Christ. It would be impossible within the limits of a single address to discuss in detail the various theories and explanations of this transcendent theme. It will suffice for the present to gather up three great messages of the cross.

1. It manifests God's character and love.

It was not the procuring cause of God's favor to lost men, but it was the direct result of divine love originating in the heart of the Father Himself. God does not love us because He died for us, but Christ died for us because God loves us. "God commendeth His love toward us in that while we were yet sinners Christ died for us." "Whom God hath set forth to be a propitiation through faith in His blood for the remission of sins that are past, through the forbearance of God, that He might be just and the justifier of him that believeth in Jesus." "God was in Christ reconciling the world unto Himself, not imputing unto men their trespasses, and hath committed unto us the word of reconciliation."

"Now then we are ambassadors for Christ, as though God did beseech you by us: we pray you in Christ's stead, be ye reconciled to God."

How clear! How unmistakable and how impressive is the attitude of God to this sinful race as presented in these Scripture passages! It is not the picture of a rigorous tyrant, the embodiment of justice and vengeance, demanding a certain price as the condition of withholding His wrath and judgment, but a loving Father who is providing all the measures so infinitely and perfectly adapted to meet the difficulties of the case and open the way for the salvation of His erring children.

There is no compromise of justice or holiness here. There is no letting down the bars of law and righteousness. There is no whitewashing of the sinner or condoning of the sin. In infinite justice and holiness, God recognized all the barriers to be overcome, and in infinite wisdom He provided for them. It would not have been proper or possible for a stranger to interpose, and even by the sacrifice of himself turn aside the judgment that man had incurred. But just as in the beginning the race had been represented in its sin by one man, Adam, its earthly head, so it was consistent and proper that in the redemption it should be represented by another man, Christ, the second Adam, its spiritual head. And so He comes as the head of our race, the second man, with the right to assume our liabilities and meet our penalties and obligations. He is sent for this very purpose by the Father. It is His own predestined provision of grace. His crucifixion is no accident of human passion and hate. But the apostle Peter gives this sublime explanation of the tragedy of the cross, "Him being delivered by the determinate council and foreknowledge of God, ye have taken and by wicked hands have crucified and slain." It was God's plan although it was man's crime.

And so we see back of the cross the figure of the Father's heart, the love that way back in Eden had cried over His fallen child, "Adam, where art thou?" and ever since has been seeking to find him, and the infinite mercy that laid upon His own Son the wrong that we had committed against our God, and thus took upon Himself our sin and met all its penalties and consequences through His great sacrifice. And now, the barriers all removed, the sin canceled, the ground of our justification perfect and complete, He stands before that cross and points to its message of love, proclaiming that He is reconciled and pleading with His dying and sinning children, "Be ye reconciled to God."

On the strength of that divine transaction we are justified in inviting every lost and sinful child of Adam's race to come back to God, for the sin question is settled and the only question on which our destiny now depends is the Son question, "What will you do with Jesus?"

2. It is a settlement of the question of sin.

Back of all the story of love and grace is the shadow of an awful problem, which infinite wisdom and holiness had to solve before the mercy of the Father's heart could find a channel for its overflow. There was the dreadful problem of sin to be solved. Love alone could not solve it, for divine righteousness must be manifested, the divine law must be vindicated, and God must be a just God as well as a Saviour. And so out of this problem have grown such words as atonement, reconciliation, redemption, ransom, propitiation, sacrifice, and the mysterious but supreme significance of the blood. We cannot ignore these figures or reason away their awful significance. It was a costly salvation, and every ransomed soul must say with the Psalmist, "There is forgiveness with Thee, that Thou mayest be feared." Perhaps we cannot better explain the philosophy of the atonement than by explaining these figures and phrases.

The idea of redemption finds its earliest and most instructive figure in the Hebrew Passover. The life of the firstborn had been forfeited, and in every Egyptian home, that forfeit was literally obeyed, and a great cry went up from the land of Egypt as the destroying angel passed by. But in the Hebrew homes, a life had been given for the firstborn, the life of a spotless lamb, of little value in itself, but of infinite worth as the type of the Lamb of God, the great Redeemer who was to come in the fullness of time. The blood of the Paschal lamb represented the life of Jesus offered as the ransom and substitute for the firstborn. Hence every firstborn among the Hebrews was the Lord's, dedicated to Him by the right of redemption.

The sprinkled blood on the doorpost simply represented the life that had been given as a ransom, and for the sake of that life, the destroying angel passed by, or more literally, as the Hebrew signifies, hovered and accepted the sacrifice with the manifestation of the divine approval, even as the Shekinah hovered over the sprinkled blood of the mercy seat. For us the significance and sublime significance of this figure is that our sinful and condemned lives have been redeemed through the vicarious offering of Jesus Christ in our stead. For the sake of that offering of infinite price, we are not only saved from condemnation but "accepted in the beloved" and "even as He."

Another term of great force and significance is the word "propitiation." Literally it means a covering. Back of it lies the figure of the mercy seat, which was called the propitiatory. This was the lid of the ark of the covenant, and if we will endeavor to make real the actual figure involved, it will bring the truth into great distinctness and beauty. In the ark of the covenant the law was deposited, the law which the people had broken and which was the witness against their sin. Above the ark the Shekinah looked down, representing the omniscient eye of divine holiness. But between the Shekinah and the ark interposed the bloody covenant or mercy seat, so that God looked down, not upon the record of their sin, but upon the blood of propitiation, and He saw not the sin but the precious blood which cleanseth from all sin. Therefore we read such expressions as this: "He hath not seen iniquity in Jacob, nor perverseness in Israel." "Blessed is the man whose transgression is forgiven, whose sin is covered." "Blessed is the man unto whom the Lord imputeth not iniquity."

The first effect of Christ's death is our justification. "Being justified freely by His grace, through the redemption that is in Christ Jesus, whom God hath set forth to be the propitiation through faith in His blood, to declare His righteousness for the remission of sins that are past, through forbearance, to declare, I say, at this time His righteousness, that He might be just and the justifier of Him that believeth in Jesus." The justification here described is not a moral change in the character of the believer, but a legal or forensic act by which he is acquitted of the guilt of sin through the offering of Jesus Christ imputed to him. This is the sense in which the Psalmist's benediction becomes true on "the man to whom the Lord imputeth not iniquity." The reason why our sin is not imputed unto us is because it has been expiated in the death of Christ, and through our union with Christ we are counted dead with Him, and as the apostle well says, "He that is dead is justified from sin." If you were executed under the law of your country for a capital crime, and by some miracle were raised from the dead, you could not be executed a second time for the same crime. You have already paid the penalty by your death. This is the position of the believer. Through the death of Christ, the Head of our humanity, we have died to law and our sin is expiated, and the new man resurrected in Christ Jesus is no longer responsible for the sins of the old man but stands justified under the decree of the throne. "Who is he that condemneth? It is Christ that died.

Who shall lay anything to the charge of God's elect? It is God that justifieth."

But the death of Christ brings us also our sanctification. Not only did He die for our past transgressions; He died for our old self-life and sinful nature. The apostle declares, "Know ye not that your old man was crucified with Christ, that the body of sin might be destroyed that ye should not henceforth serve sin?" The new created spirit is freed from the power as well as the poverty of sin, and through the indwelling life of Christ and the power of the Holy Ghost, it can take the victorious position of Romans 8:2, 4: "The law of the Spirit of life in Christ Jesus hath made me free from the law of sin and death, so that the righteousness of the law might be fulfilled in us, who walk not after the flesh, but after the Spirit."

3. It is the secret of the victory of the life of love over the life of self. The real essence of all sin is self-love. "God is love," and selfishness is the antagonist of love. The death of Christ has set the standard of love for the universe of God. Henceforth holy character is summed up in self-sacrifice and service. "We thus judge," the apostle declares, "that if one died for all, then all died, and He died for all that they which live should not henceforth live unto themselves but unto Him that died for them and rose again." No man can look on Calvary with an honest gaze and see

"His dying crimson like a robe, spread o'er His body on the tree" and henceforth dare to live on the old plane of selfishness. If you are living on that plane, you have not connected with Calvary, you have not got the spirit of the cross; you have not learned the lesson, "The Son of man came not to be ministered unto, but to minister and to give His life a ransom for many. He that saveth his life shall lose it; he that loseth his life for

Back To Calvary

My sake shall keep it unto life eternal." Redemption means consecration.

An African slave, named Garra, was about to be executed by a cruel chief because he had displeased him. An Englishman, who was a Christian, entreated for his life. The proud chief replied, "Libo has gold, slaves and everything you could give him. Nothing can persuade him to give up his offending slave. Libo wants blood." And so he ordered the slave to be bound and the archers to prepare for his execution. Suddenly the Englishman threw himself in front of Garra, and the first arrow pierced his arm. He sprang forward before the chief and said, "I give you blood, my blood, and I claim his liberty." The chief was amazed, for he never had seen anything like this, and he was compelled to yield. But now the turn of the slave came. There he is at the feet of his deliverer and crying, "Oh, son of love, Garra thanks you with his life which you have bought and which he gives back to you," and all through the jungles of Africa the grateful slave followed his new master. No service was too hard, no sacrifice too great, for he had been redeemed, and his life and love belonged to his redeemer. Surely we behold that

"Crimson like a robe

Flow o'er His body on the tree,

Then am I dead to all the world,

And all the world is dead me.

Were the whole realm of nature mine,

That were a present far too small;

Love so amazing, so divine,

Demands my heart, my life, my all."

CHAPTER VII

THE GOSPEL OF JUSTIFICATION

> "Being justified freely by His grace through the redemption that is in Christ Jesus . . . that He might be just, and the justifier of him which believeth in Jesus."
>
> (Romans 3:24–26).

THERE is such a thing in human courts as condemning a man to save him. A wise lawyer, when he perceives that his client cannot prove his innocence, will always advise him to "plead guilty" and then throw himself upon the clemency of the court. Mercy cannot be exercised until guilt is confessed.

And so God has to prove man guilty in order to save him. The two first chapters of Romans are God's fearful indictment against the Gentile and the Jew, and He finally sums up the whole case by pronouncing both Jew and Gentile under sin, and laying them prostrate and guilty before God, with every mouth stopped and every excuse silenced.

Then He begins to reveal the plan of salvation, through the atonement and righteousness of Jesus Christ.

Once in a French prison, a Russian prince, through the prerogative of Napoleon, was permitted to pardon a convict. So he proceeded to question the different men he met, with a view to finding someone worthy of his clemency. But every man professed to be entirely innocent, and, indeed, greatly wronged and unjustly punished.

At last, he found one man who was qualified to receive forgiveness—the only guilty man in all the prison—and he had nothing to plead for himself, but frankly confessed his unworthiness, and acknowledged that he deserved all the punishment he had received.

The prince was deeply touched by his humility and penitence, and he said to him: "I have brought you forgiveness, and in the name of your emperor, I pronounce you a free man. You are the only man I have found in all this place ready to acknowledge his guilt and take the place where mercy could be extended to him."

This is the place that God is bringing men to, and when He gets them there, He loves to lift them up to His bosom and pronounce upon them, not the sentence of condemnation, but of acquittal and forgiveness.

In the beautiful allegory of Mansoul, written by John Bunyan, we have an account of the surrender of the garrison to King Immanuel. They resisted as long as they could, but beleaguered and starving, they were finally compelled to give up the conflict and yield themselves to the mercy of their conqueror.

His answer was that every one of them must come forth into his presence with chains upon their necks and cry, "We are guilty, and worthy of death." And so, in great humility and fear, they marched forth from the city gates and threw themselves at his feet. They expected the severest punishment, for they had resisted to the bitter end, and knew that they deserved nothing but death.

But as soon as they had echoed their humble confession, King Immanuel ordered the trumpet of the herald to proclaim, in the hearing of all his camp, that they were freely pardoned through his mercy and restored to his favor, that their city should be rebuilt, should become his own royal capital and be treated with peculiar favor, and they should be adopted as the children of the king.

They were overwhelmed with astonishment, and burst out into tears of gratitude and shouts of praise.

Yes, this is the glorious paradox of Divine mercy. "God hath concluded all under sin, that He might have mercy upon all."

I. THE NATURE OF JUSTIFICATION

There is much misunderstanding about the term and the experience. It is essentially different from regeneration. That means a change of heart and character. Justification is a change of our relations with God. Literally the word means to *declare righteous*. It is the judicial act by which God acquits the sinner of all guilt and gives him the standing of a righteous man, although personally he may have been the chief of sinners. It is called a forensic act, that is, the act of a judge, a declaration from the forum or judgment seat. While every justified man has the experience of regeneration and a change of heart, yet justification itself does not refer to that but to the act of God in dealing with our sins and putting them away by the verdict of His grace. It is more than forgiveness. It puts the sinner in the place of complete discharge and perfect righteousness. He is in as good a position as if he had already been punished for his own sins, indeed, in as good a position as if he had performed the acts of righteousness which Christ has done in his stead, and which are imputed to him through faith in Jesus. "God justifieth the ungodly." "By Him all that believe are justified from all things from which they could not be justified by the law of Moses." The apostle Paul illustrates the doctrine of justification from the case of Abraham. "If Abraham were justified by works, he hath whereof to glory, but not before God. For what saith the Scripture? Abraham believed God, and it was reckoned unto him for righteousness. Now to him that worketh, the reward is not reckoned as of grace, but as of debt, but to him that worketh not, but believeth on him that justifieth the ungodly, his faith is reckoned for righteousness" (Rom. 4:2-5). He then proceeds to further illustrate it from the case of David. "Even as David also pronounceth blessing upon the man, unto whom God reckoneth righteousness without work, saying, Blessed is the man whose iniquity is forgiven, whose sin is covered, and to whom the Lord imputeth not iniquity." We cannot better sum up the definition of justification than by quoting a familiar sentence: "Justification is an act of God's free grace, wherein He freely pardoneth all our sins and accepteth us as righteous in His sight, only for the righteousness of Christ imputed unto us and received by faith alone."

II. THE SCOPE OF JUSTIFICATION

The purpose of Christ's work was not merely to relieve man from a dangerous situation, but much more to reveal God in the highest attitude and aspect of justice, wisdom and love, not only for His own glory, but also for the highest dignity and security of redeemed man. God has made the plan of salvation more a matter of justice and righteousness than even of grace and mercy, so that all through this Epistle to the Romans, the term "righteousness" predominates in describing the plan of salvation.

This is the difference between Christianity and all human religions. They try to bring God down to the level of man's sinfulness and adjust the moral scale to the low standard of man's actual condition.

God's plan of salvation is the opposite of this and aims to bring man's condition up to the level of Divine law. Not one principle of justice is compromised, not one jot or tittle of the law is modified or evaded. Every requirement of justice is met, and when man is saved, he is enabled to stand without a blush of shame and claim his acquittal from the very decree of eternal justice, as much as from the gentle bosom of forgiving mercy.

I remember a noble friend of twenty years ago, a businessman of high standing among his fellows. I often used to mark his manly bearing, the high and noble dignity of his face and his walk, and the profound respect in which he was held by all his acquaintances. One day I learned the secret.

He had failed in business long years before, and was offered a settlement by his creditors involving a compromise of his debts. This he would not accept, but asked only for time and opportunity to pay every dollar, with interest, and he went back again to the struggle of life to do this and never ceased from his high purpose until he had redeemed his pledge and met the claims of every man to the last cent. Then he walked the streets of that city with the majesty of a king among men. He was not forgiven; he was justified.

This is what God aims to do in the plan of salvation. He does not want to pass over the transgressions of the sinner by a mere act of kindness. He wants us to know that every sin has been actually dealt with, punished and ended, and that we are in just the same position with the law of God as if we had never sinned, nay, better still, as if we had kept every command of the law blamelessly. Through our great Substitute, sin has not only been met and punished, but, through His atonement, we are made blameless, and the same as if we had suffered ourselves.

The word *justify* means to "declare righteous." It does not necessarily imply that the one declared righteous *is* righteous. In fact, it is assumed, in the case of the sinner, that he is *not* righteous. It is the ungodly that God justifies, but he is recognized, not in himself, but in the person of his substitute, the Lord Jesus Christ, and His righteousness is regarded as ours, and for His sake we are treated even as He.

The life which He laid down is accepted for our forfeited life, and the obedience which He rendered is accounted as our obedience. "He was made sin for us, who knew no sin, that we might be the righteousness of God in Him," and so the sinner can look in the face of even the Holy Ghost and say, "There is, therefore, now no condemnation to them that are in Christ Jesus." He can face the great accuser and cry, "Who is he that condemneth? It is Christ that died." He may look even in the face of his conscience, and at the victims of his very crimes, and with a heart breaking with humble contrition, he can still cry, "Who shall lay anything to the charge of God's elect? It is God that justifieth."

This is set forth by three terms that are very significant. The first is "redemption." "The redemption that is in Christ Jesus."

This denotes a definite transaction through which we are purchased back from a condition of liability to punishment, through a price, or ransom, definitely paid.

The salvation of man is based upon a very definite transaction between the Father and the Son—the covenant of redemption entered into in the ages past, and actually fulfilled by the Lord Jesus Christ, when He became incarnate on earth and died on Calvary. The Father stipulated in this covenant that, for certain conditions, He would give to His Son the eternal salvation of

His people. These conditions involved the offering up of His life on the cross, His perfect obedience and all the mediatorial acts which our Saviour is now fulfilling.

These conditions have been absolutely fulfilled, and now it is a matter of redemption right for God to forgive the believer and save the penitent and trusting soul. Therefore, we read that "If we confess our sins, God is faithful and just to forgive us our sins and to cleanse us from all unrighteousness." It is a matter of righteousness for Him to do so. So, again, we are told, "To as many as received Him, to them gave He the right to become the sons of God, even to as many as believed in His name." "Thus we have redemption through His blood, even the forgiveness of sins, according to the riches of His grace."

The second of these terms is "propitiation." This word literally means "covering." It is also used as a corresponding word in the Old Testament to signify cleansing. The literal idea, however, is that of covering. It suggests the mercy seat in the tabernacle. The position of the mercy seat was strikingly significant of its spiritual reference. It was the covering of the ark. Underneath it, and within the ark, lay the tables of the law, which man had broken, and which witnessed against his sin.

Over it hovered the Shekinah, symbolical of God's all-seeing eye. That eye was looking down upon the ark. Had it seen only that broken law and the sin against which it testified, it could only have flashed its holy fire against the transgressors, and could not have rested in covenant love upon the worshippers in that sacred place.

But it did not see the sin at all, for between the ark and the Shekinah was the mercy seat, the covering lid of pure gold always sprinkled with the blood of atonement. God saw only the blood, and it covered the sin. And so we read such words as these: "Blessed is the man whose transgression is forgiven, whose sin is covered." "He hath not seen iniquity in Jacob, nor perverseness in Israel." "Christ is the propitiation for our sins, and not for ours only, but also for the sins of the whole world."

The third term used is "His blood." Of course this refers to His death. The blood is the life, and the offering of Christ's blood always expresses His vicarious sacrifice for sin. The ransom was His life; the propitiation is His blood. He has stood between us and the just consequences of our guilt, and "The Lord hath laid on Him the iniquity of us all." "Who His own self bare our sins in His own body on the tree, that we, being dead to sins, should live unto righteousness: by whose stripes ye were healed."

This is the core of Christianity. This is the essence of the Gospel. This is the ground of our justification. God has set forth Jesus Christ so emphatically that His great atonement cannot be misunderstood or evaded by any honest mind, and He is the propitiation through His blood, by whom God can "declare His righteousness for the remission of sins that are past, through the forbearance of God . . . that He might be just, and the justifier of him which believeth in Jesus."

III. THE FINALITY OF JUSTIFICATION

"For the remission of sins that are past, through the forbearance of God."

The language here is very expressive, and it intimates that in the past, and up to the time of Christ's death, God was forbearing with sin but it was not settled for.

There are two Greek words used, expressive of the two thoughts that stand forth here in bold relief. One is *paresis*, the other *aphesis*. *Paresis* means to "pass by," *aphesis* to "put away." Under the Old Testament, it was *paresis;* under the New, it is *aphesis*. Then, it was forbearance. Now, it is remission. Then,

God overlooked sin, not lightly, nor capriciously, but in view of the settlement that was to be made by Christ on Calvary, and which was recognized as already accomplished through "the Lamb slain from the foundation of the world." But the ransom was not literally paid, and so God dealt with men in forbearance and in anticipation of the coming atonement.

Christ had, as it were, given His promissory note for the payment of the ransom, and God accepted it, and dealt with believers under the old covenant, under the assumption that it would be paid. Christ redeemed it on Calvary, and thus it was taken out of the way, nailed to His cross, and the full efficacy of His atonement became real. Sin was now put away, canceled, annihilated.

He had come to finish transgression, to make an end of sin, to bring in everlasting righteousness, and now we who accept the Lord Jesus are not only taken on probation, and dealt with as objects of forbearance, but we are wholly justified, we are eternally saved, and received into the fellowship and communion of God, even as His own beloved Son, in whom we are accepted.

"He that heareth My Word, and believeth on Him that sent Me," Jesus said, "hath everlasting life, and shall not come into condemnation, but hath passed from death unto life." "My sheep hear My voice, and I know them, and they follow Me; and I give unto them eternal life, and they shall never perish, neither shall any man pluck them out of My hand."

The work of Jesus Christ is complete, final, eternal. "By one offering He hath perfected forever them that are sanctified." "Now once in the end of the world hath He appeared to put away sin by the sacrifice of Himself." "And unto them that look for Him shall He appear the second time without sin unto salvation." Is not this a glorious redemption, a divine foundation, a strong consolation, a Rock of Ages?

Is not this a better resting place for your confidence and hope than all your transitory feelings and variable experiences? Is not this a blessed place to rest when the brain gets clouded and the heart gets sad and cold, and the adversary hurls his fiery darts into the self-accusing conscience?

Well I remember a dear old saint who had brought scores of souls to Christ in a long and useful Christian life. But as her sun began to go down, clouds gathered around her horizon, her brain grew weak, her faith became dimmed, and she thought she was no longer useful to Jesus Christ and He no longer wanted her. Blessed soul! How sweet it was to tell her that her salvation rested upon the immutable Word of God, and that she was safe in Jesus Christ, the Rock of Ages that nothing could ever shake!

O beloved, let us be sure that we are fast anchored to this eternal Rock—the redemption of our Lord Jeus Christ.

IV. THE CONDITIONS OF JUSTIFICATION

"Being justified freely by His grace." This is almost a redundancy, for "freely" and "grace" mean the same. But the design of the writer is to express the idea with all possible emphasis. This salvation, all the way through, is the gift of God. We cannot earn it, deserve it, nor work it out ourselves. We must receive it, from beginning to end, directly from our Father's hands on equal terms of mercy and personal worthlessness. Our works, experiences, and usefulness have nothing whatever to do in securing our salvation.

There is no difference in the standing of all men at the gateway of life. "All have sinned and come short of the glory of God; being justified freely by His grace," and whatever else we have along with this—whatever of holiness or usefulness God has permitted any of us to enjoy—this also is through the riches of His grace. "What hast thou that thou hast not received?" Even Paul had to say, in speaking of his salvation, "I obtained mercy," and then he added, of his subsequent career, "The grace of God was exceeding abundant, with faith and love which is in Christ Jesus."

It is true there is a great difference at the end, but there is none at the beginning. On equal terms we enter the gates of mercy, all alike condemned, and then we are permitted, in the great goodness of God, to strive for the crown of recompense and press toward the goal in the race for victory.

It is just the same as if, in some great public school, free admission should be given to all who applied, irrespective of their personal circumstances and merits, but after they are admitted freely to the school, there are prizes given to the boys according to their diligence and proficiency in the various studies.

So God takes us all in as helpless, worthless sinners, but after we enter the school of Christ as the beneficiaries of His grace, we are invited and permitted to press forward to the higher rewards which He offers to the diligent and faithful.

But even the power to gain the reward and strive for the mastery is still the gift of grace and infinite mercy. And so it is all of grace, through the purchase of Christ's precious blood and the gift of the Father's sovereign love.

"The righteousness of God which is by faith of Jesus Christ unto all and upon all them that believe; for there is no difference"; and again, in the twenty-seventh verse, "The law of faith" is spoken of. This is the principle underlying the whole Gospel system. Every blessing must be received by faith. This is the only way in which a gift can be received. There is no merit in an act of faith. It is simply taking what God gives with thanks and trust.

It is certainly a very blessed act, because when the heart receives the love and grace of God, it exercises a most blessed influence on our life character, but in itself it is not a work of merit, but simply the means by which we receive what God has to give.

It is the law of faith. It is the principle on which God is acting with men. "Without faith it is impossible to please God." Let us accept it as the principle and law of our lives, as it is the law of God's administration for sinful men.

God has the boundless riches of His grace for the most lost and sinful, if they will only accept the gift and receive it by simple trust, but we shall be lost by unbelief much more certainly than by the darkest crime of which human nature is capable.

It is said that once an English landlord, in order to teach his peasantry the lesson of trusting God, offered on a certain day to pay the debts of all his tenantry if they would bring him a statement of all their debts and accept as a gift his generous bounty.

The morning came, and he waited in his office until the hour of noon, according to the announcement which he had widely published. The people gathered in curious knots around the street, and wondered what it all meant. They could not understand such liberal generosity, and they waited for someone to go in and prove that he really meant it, and then they would all go in for their share. But the day wore on, and none of them seemed willing to go in.

At last an aged couple came along, and tottering up the steps, approached the door. The people outside crowded around them and said eagerly, "Now be sure to hurry through, and tell us all about it."

The old couple went in, and the landlord received them very kindly, looked over their statement, paid the debts gladly, and then asked them if there was anything more he could do for their comfort. He said that he had a certain sum of money that he intended to spend in this way, but none of the people seemed to want it. So he gave the old couple enough to buy a little cottage, and provided for all the needs of their closing days. They poured out their thanks with tears of joy.

When they arose to go, he detained them a few moments, chatting pleasantly with them, until the clock struck twelve; then he arose, opened the door for them to pass out, and said: "The time that I appointed in the announcement has now expired, and other engagements call me away." He bade them "good-bye," and as they tottered feebly down the steps, the crowd eagerly pressed about them, asking, "Did he really pay your debts?" "Did he mean it?" The old people looked at them with astonishment in their faces, and said, "Why, of course he did."

The people now hastened to the door, anxious to enter, but before they reached it, he had passed out, and with a polite bow, hurried away, saying, "Good morning, neighbours, I am sorry you were too late, but another engagement calls me away. The time has expired, the opportunity has passed." Oh, how sorry they were that they had not trusted his word!

The next Sabbath, as he talked with them in his mission hall about the promises of Jesus, and what they mean, many hearts realized as they had never done before the folly and wickedness of unbelief, and the blessedness of trusting God, and of remembering, "He means just what He says."

V. THE EFFECTS OF JUSTIFICATION

This faith is not a mere intellectual assent to the truths of the Bible, but a living confidence in God through the Lord Jesus Christ. "The word is nigh thee, even in thy mouth, and in thy heart . . . that if thou shalt confess with thy mouth the Lord Jesus, and shalt believe in thine heart that God hath raised him from the dead, thou shalt be saved. For with the heart man believeth unto righteousness" (Rom. 10:8–10).

First, it brings our discharge from guilt and condemnation. "Being now justified by His blood, we shall be saved from wrath through Him" (Rom. 5:9). "There is therefore now no condemnation to them which are in Christ Jesus" (Rom. 8:1). "Verily, verily, I say unto you, he that heareth My word, and believeth on Him that sent Me, hath everlasting life, and shall not come into judgment, but is passed from death unto life" (John 5:24). "Who shall lay any thing to the charge of God's elect? It is God that justifieth. Who is he that condemneth? It is Christ that died, yea rather, that is risen again, who is even at the right hand of God, who also maketh intercession for us" (Rom. 8:33–34).

Second, it makes us accepted as righteous through the imputed righteousness of Christ. "For as by one man's disobedience many were made sinners, so by the obedience of one shall many be made righteous" (Rom. 5:19). "He hath made us accepted in the beloved" (Eph. 1:6). "This is His name whereby He shall be called, the Lord our Righteousness." "This is the name wherewith she shall be called, the Lord our Righteousness" (Jer. 23:6; 33:16). The bride receives the name of the Bridegroom, and that name is Righteousness.

Third, it brings us peace with God. "Therefore being justified by faith, we have peace with God through our Lord Jesus

Christ" (Rom. 5:1). First, there is the peace of reconciliation, and secondly, there is the peace of rest and consolation.

Fourth, it brings us the right to the inheritance of life eternal. "That being justified by His grace, we should be made heirs according to the hope of eternal life" (Titus 3:7). "Moreover whom He did predestinate, them He also called, and whom He called, them He also justified, and whom He justified, them He also glorified" (Rom. 8:30). "For the judgment came of one unto condemnation, but the free gift came of many trespasses unto justification, for if by one man's offence death reigned by one; much more they which receive abundance of grace and of the gift of righteousness shall reign in life by one, Jesus Christ" (Rom. 5:16–17).

Objections have been offered to the doctrine of justification, especially on the ground that it leads to license and encourages lawlessness and disobedience. The Roman Catholic Church holds that justification is not wholly by grace and by faith, but partly by works, and quotes the argument of James to the effect that Abraham was justified by works. The answer of the Reformed leaders has always been that James was talking about a different kind of justification, not the justification of a sinner, but the manifestation of a true believer and the vindication of the reality and sincerity of his faith by consistent works. The works do not have any part in his justification before God, but they do in his vindication before men and prove the reality of his professions. The great principle involved is the distinction between law and grace. Are men really influenced to holiness by the fear of punishment? Or are they attracted to it by the love of Christ and the sense of forgiveness and salvation? The law had its day and failed to make men better, but the grace of Jesus Christ not only saves but sanctifies all who truly receive it.

One is reminded of the simple testimony of a common soldier. When the Duke of Wellington was about to pronounce a sentence of death on a confirmed deserter, the General was deeply moved and said, "I am extremely sorry to have to pass this severe sentence, but we have tried everything, and all our discipline and penalties have failed to improve this man who otherwise is a brave and good soldier." And then he gave an opportunity for his comrades to speak for him. Instantly one honest fellow stood up and with great deference asked if he might speak; and when permitted, he added, "Please, Your Excellency, there is one thing you have never tried, and that is forgiving him." The good Duke was touched and consented to try the new way, and it is said that thereafter he never had a truer soldier in the Peninsula.

> "Law and terrors do but harden
> All the while they work alone,
> But a sense of blood-bought pardon
> Soon dissolves a heart of stone."

CHAPTER VIII

FREE GRACE

"I marvel that ye are so soon removed from Him that called you into the grace of Christ unto another gospel" (Galatians 1:6).

"Stand fast therefore in the liberty wherewith Christ hath made us free, and be not entangled again with the yoke of bondage" (Galatians 5:1).

THE Galatians were the Celts of western Asia, like the French, the Irish and Scottish Highlanders of our day; a high-spirited, impulsive people, as quick to be perverted as they had been to be converted at the preaching of Paul. They had received him on his first visit with intense enthusiasm "as an angel of God, even as Christ Jesus," and "if it had been possible, they would have plucked out their own eyes and given them to him." But now they have turned back at the bidding of false teachers and just as promptly gone after "the weak and beggarly elements, whereunto ye desire again to be in bondage. Ye observe days and months and times and years." "Ye did run well; who did hinder you that ye should not obey the truth?" They had fallen into the hands of the high church or ritualistic party of that day. It is the old and favorite counterfeit of the enemy which again today is sweeping so many by a resistless current on to the inevitable shores of Romanism, a desire for ceremony and outward form instead of spirituality and holiness. This was the delusion which had drawn away the once fervid and evangelical churches of Galatia. These false teachers were trying to draw them back to Judaism, the ceremonial law, the rite of circumcision and the bondage of the past. And in order to fortify their position, they had persuaded the Galatians that Paul had no authority to preach the Gospel to them, that he was inferior to the other apostles, and that James and Peter were the true leaders of the church and the supreme authorities on matters of Church law and practice.

Paul, therefore, is compelled to vindicate his apostleship, and so he rehearses the story of his call and ministry, and reminds them that his authority is not of man, nor by man, but directly from God the Father and the Lord Jesus Christ. He reminds them of his independent stand with the other apostles and of his direct commission to the Gentiles, which even the apostles themselves freely admitted. He tells them also of his firm attitude when the Judaising party demanded that Titus the Gentile should be circumcised, to whom he yielded "no, not for an hour; that the truth of the Gospel might continue." Nay, further he reminds them that when Peter became inconsistent, and after having received the Gentiles through the deeper teaching of the Spirit, afterwards went back through fear of the Jews and resumed his old conservative and exclusive attitude, drawing away even Barnabas with him, he declares, "When I saw that they walked not uprightly according to the truth, I withstood Peter to the face, because he was to be blamed."

Having thus vindicated his own apostleship and proved his consistent attitude in relation to the Gospel, he proceeds to unfold his great argument for free grace, and against the false teachers and Judaising elements of the day. The result is one of the most precious of the New Testament epistles of which the keynote throughout is the word "free grace," especially as we trace it in our salvation, our sanctification and our spirit toward others.

I. WHAT WE MEAN BY FREE GRACE

1. Grace is the divine goodness with special reference to the unworthy and the helpless. It is not love to the good, but to the bad. There is something in God which can love the unlovely and the evil, and can take hold of wrong and by the power of His grace lift it and to the right and even turn the curse into a blessing. "How wonderful," said one, after speaking of the grace of God to poor sinners. "No," said a poor slave, who had lately been saved; "It is not wonderful at all, it is just like Him." And yet it is so unlike us that the natural heart cannot understand it.

On the Cornish coast two fishermen were on unfriendly terms. One was a rude and most ungodly man, who took every opportunity to injure and insult the other, who was a Christian, even destroying his fishing nets under some pretext of trespassing on his grounds. One stormy day the fishing boat of the former was drifting out to sea and would certainly have been lost had not the other leaped into the surf and by desperate exertions rescued it. As he slowly drew it to its moorings and came ashore, the owner had come out of an ale house and was standing with sulky mien on the shore. Too rude to thank him, he looked up with a sulky glance and said, "Why did you do that? But how could you do it after the way I have treated you?"

"Why," said the other, "I couldn't help it."

"What are you?" said the first.

"I am a Christian," he answered.

"Well," said the other, "you are the first I have met." That is grace, the sort of love that can't help blessing them that curse us and doing good to the unthankful and undeserving. The apostle has defined it in another of his epistles thus: "God, who is rich in mercy, for His great love wherewith He loved us, even when we were dead in sins." "For God commendeth His love toward us, in that, while we were yet sinners, Christ died for us."

2. Salvation is the gift of God's free grace. It is not deserved or earned by works, but it is the bestowment of God's sovereign grace. "The gift of God is eternal life through Jesus Christ our Lord." "By grace are ye saved through faith, and that not of yourselves. It is the gift of God; not of works lest any man should boast." The only terms on which we can have salvation at all is by taking the place of the sinner and accepting the mercy of God, for Christ's sake.

3. This grace is purchased through the ransom of Christ's blood. While free to us, it was most costly to Him, and the price paid was His own life. "Who gave Himself for our sins, that He might deliver us from this present evil world, according to the will of God and our Father" (Gal. 1:4). "Christ hath redeemed us from the curse of the law, being made a curse for us" (Gal. 3:13).

4. The grace of God for Christ's sake justifies us and puts us in the same position as if we had never sinned. It is not mere scant deliverance from condemnation, but it is complete and honorable justification. It is not our discharge because the jury has failed to agree upon a conviction, or the executive has determined upon a pardon; but it is a decree of the supreme court of the universe proclaiming us faultless and blameless and putting us in as good a position as the Lord Jesus Christ Himself, our Surety and Substitute.

5. But grace has yet another direction in the sinner's salvation. "He called me by His grace" (Gal. 1:15). It was the grace of God that brought Paul even to know and receive God's grace. Vainly for him had the gift been offered and the ransom paid unless grace had also stooped so low as to reach him in his unbelief and win him in his alienation and sin. For Paul had been a bitter enemy of the grace of God, had rejected the Saviour and was doing all in his power to oppose the Gospel and destroy its followers, and at the very moment of his conversion was in the high tide of his rebellion and unbelief. But the grace of God struck him down in the blossom of his sin and compelled him to accept its proffered love. And so Paul became a captive of grace and never tired of celebrating the love that when we were enemies reconciled us to God. We may think that we may have had a different history and that we were quite as earnest in seeking God as He in seeking us, but when the whole story is told, it will be found at last that there is not much difference between the best of us and the blunt Scotchman, who, when asked how his conversion came about, said that it took two to do it, one was God and the other was himself. When his good Calvinistic pastor asked him how he could claim any part of it, he answered, "God drew me, and I resisted all I could." That is about the most we can say for our part. "By the grace of God I am what I am," was the testimony of Paul, and the epitaph on the monument of William Carey may well take us all in:

> "A worthless, weak and helpless worm,
> On Thy kind arms I fall.
> Be Thou my perfect righteousness,
> My Saviour and my All."

II. HIS ARGUMENT FOR FREE GRACE

1. He proves it from the covenant with Abraham. "Even as Abraham believed God, and it was accounted to him for righteousness." And the Scripture foreseeing that God would justify the heathen through faith preached before the Gospel unto Abraham, saying, "In thee shall all nations be blessed. So then they which be of faith are blessed with faithful Abraham" (Gal. 3:6–9). The authority of Abraham, their father, was supreme with every Jew, and therefore Paul appeals to it and reminds them that the covenant of salvation made with Abraham for himself and his seed was purely one of faith and grace. For even in Genesis we are told that Abraham's faith "was counted to him for righteousness" (Gen. 15:6). Then later in the chapter, Paul reminds them that the covenant with Abraham was made 430 years before the law on Sinai, and, therefore, that later law could not "disannul" or "make the promise of none effect" (Gal. 3:17). The covenant with Abraham was an everlasting covenant and its very principle was free grace and not works, faith and not personal merit. And so all believers still are recognized as the children of Abraham and coinheritors with him of the grace of God.

2. His next argument for free grace is founded on the law of Moses. For even the law, he tells us, had in it the principle of grace. The very object of the law was to convict men of sin and so throw them upon the mercy of God. "Is the law then against the promises of God? God forbid. But the Scripture hath concluded all under sin, that the promise by faith of Jesus Christ might be given to them that believe" (Gal. 3:21–22). "Wherefore," he adds, introducing a fine figure, "the law was our schoolmaster to bring us unto Christ, that we might be justified by faith" (Gal. 3:24). The Greek word is "pedagogue." Now the pedagogue was not a schoolmaster

exactly, but the manservant who took the children to school and delivered them over to the schoolmaster who took charge of their studies. Christ is the real Teacher, and the law was just the servant to conduct us to Christ. When Christ comes, the work of the law is accomplished. "But after that faith is come, we are no longer under a schoolmaster, for ye are all the children of God by faith in Christ Jesus." The law never was intended to save men, but to convince them of their need of a Saviour and point forward to Him who was to be the Redeemer of men.

In the next paragraph, the apostle uses still another figure to explain the place of the law. It is the figure of the minor, the child underage who is under tutors and governors until he reaches his majority. "Even so we," he says, "were in bondage under the elements of the world, but when the fulness of the time was come, God sent forth His Son, born of a woman, made under the law, to redeem them that were under the law, that we might receive the adoption of sons. Because ye are sons, God hath sent forth the Spirit of His Son into your hearts, crying, Abba Father. Wherefore thou art no more a servant, but a son; and if a son, then an heir of God through Christ" (Gal. 4:1-7). And so the law leads on to the Gospel, and the Gospel is liberty, the freedom of the Father's house, the filial spirit, the privileges of a happy child, and if we return to the law, we must set back the hands of the clock of time more than three thousand years, and go back to Sinai and the infancy and minority of the children of God.

3. His next argument is the allegory of Ishmael and Isaac (Gal. 4:22-31). Hagar, the bondwoman, represents the law, and Ishmael, her son, the flesh. For the law can only produce the flesh. Our best efforts even in the direction of righteousness end only in self-righteousness, and we must die to our goodness, quite as much as our badness, before we can enter

the kingdom of heaven. On the other hand, Sarah represents the Gospel and the covenant of grace, while Isaac, her son, is the type of the life of the Spirit which is the offspring of grace. Just as Ishmael persecuted Isaac, so that flesh lusts against the spirit. Ishmael cannot be improved. He must be cast out. But you cannot get rid of Ishmael alone. You must cast out both the bondwoman and her son. The spirit of legality must go with the flesh. Free grace alone can bring forth the new life, and under its nourishing influence alone can the spiritual life be educated and matured. The law in every form, whether it be the ceremonial law, the moral law or the penances, tortures and struggles of conscience and self-effort of the natural man, can only end in failure and in some other form of fleshly life. "Sin shall not have dominion over you: for ye are not under the law, but under grace."

III. THE REASONS WHY THE APOSTLE CONTENDS SO EARNESTLY FOR FREE GRACE

Are the doctrines of evangelical religion so supremely important? Are we justified in contending so earnestly for the faith once delivered unto the saints? Have much men as Mr. Spurgeon, Dr. Bonar and the spiritual leaders of our time cause to fear the downgrade movement which is carrying so large a part of the Church of today into ethical culture, rationalism and Christian socialism, preaching a Christ without a cross? Have we reason to dread the subtle influence of such teachers as Mr. Herron, such stories as "In His Steps," beautiful in their theories of an ideal Christ-life, but like cut flowers that have no root? Certainly Paul had no sentimental weakness about the matter. The language he uses is uncompromising and unmistakable. "If I or an angel from heaven preach unto you any other gospel," he says, "let him be accursed." It is not merely a matter of difference of opinion. It is a matter of life and death to preach the pure Gospel of Jesus Christ and nothing else and nothing less.

1. Nothing else is worthy of God. The glory of Christianity is the sovereign grace from which it sprang, and no loyal Christian heart will abate aught of the glory due to the Father's love and the Saviour's cross.

2. It is the only salvation that is adapted to fallen man. Nothing but mercy can meet the needs of the worthless and the helpless. Because God expects nothing of us, therefore the worst and weakest of us may hope and trust. "It took me half a lifetime," says a distinguished writer, "to find out three things; namely, first, that I couldn't do anything to save myself; secondly, that God did not expect me to do anything; and third, that Christ has done all for me, and I have only to accept Him and thank Him for the free gift of eternal life."

3. Free grace is the only thing that can make men holy. Instead of encouraging men to sin, it inspires them to love and serve God. To a true nature, love is always a higher inspiration than slavish fear. God trusts us, thinks His best thoughts of us, refuses to think evil of us, and encourages us to think of ourselves accordingly. It is His love that constrains us to goodness and lifts us to love and grateful obedience. Even when we abuse God's liberty by falling into sin, His grace overrules it to teach us by discipline the bitterness of sin and the better way of loving obedience. John Ruskin tells us that his earliest recollection of youthful liberty is of sitting on his mother's knee as she was preparing tea in the glowing urn which stood on the table steaming with boiling water, while the nurse stood by. Little John gazed a while at the burnished brass and the pretty clouds of steam and insisted on reaching out his little hand and touching the urn. His mother tried to keep him back, but he grew rebellious. "Let

him touch it," said the nurse, "it will do him good." And so the mother gave him the coveted liberty. There was a sudden cry, and speaking of it afterwards, John says, "That was the last time for many years that I remember asking to have my own way." So God can sanctify to us even our own abuse of free grace. He will let you disobey Him if you will. He will let you sin if you want to. But as you think of His love and find by experience the bitterness of sin, the sweetness of obedience, you do not want to sin; you do not want to abuse so kind a Friend. His gentleness makes you good and gentle too.

John Wesley and Joseph Bradford had a severe quarrel which separated them for some days. Meeting shortly afterwards, John Wesley asked Joseph Bradford, "Don't you want to ask my forgiveness, Joseph?"

"No," said Bradford.

"Well," said Wesley, "I want to ask yours." And the two friends fell into each other's arms. Humility and grace had conquered as they ever will. It is thus that God treats the rebel and the sinner. Shall we be worthy of His grace? Shall we accept His generous love and let it lift us to higher things? Shall we stop thinking hard of ourselves until we end by thinking hard of Him? Shall we take the place the Father gives the prodigal, not the kitchen and the servant's place, but the best robe, the ring, the feast, the Father's heart and go forth to live as we often sing:

"Oh, the love that sought me!

"Oh, the blood that bought me!

Oh, the grace that brought me to the fold!

Wondrous grace that brought me to the fold!"

www.ingramcontent.com/pod-product-compliance
Lightning Source LLC
Chambersburg PA
CBHW031410040426
42444CB00005B/495